CREATIVITY
ACTIVATED

CREATIVITY
ACTIVATED

Science-Informed Tools to Upgrade Joy & Amplify Your Potential

CHRIS LUMRY

Creativity Activated: Science-Informed Tools to Upgrade Joy & Amplify Your Potential
© Copyright 2023 by Chris Lumry
Written by Chris Lumry
Published by OneStepGrowth LLC
Book Cover Design by Hayley Janzen, Chloe Wengerd, and Chris Lumry
Book Editing and Formatting: Hayley Janzen, Eline Millenaar de Guzman, Aristomelia Vidal, and Chris Lumry
Printed in the United States of America

ISBN: 979-8-9863328-1-9

PRAISE FOR CREATIVITY ACTIVATED & CREATIVITY UNLOCKED

"Building new mindsets for creativity helped me persevere in the music industry. Places that were once obstacles became opportunities. Instead of waiting for doors to open, I started creating my own around my passion for food, including Hale's Kitchen. This has launched my music onto bigger platforms than I had dreamed possible."

- Rachel, Musician

"Creativity Unlocked breathed life into my work and helped me over a hurdle. I highly recommend for anyone interested in connecting their heart to their work, because all work is creative."

- Jesse, Author

"[These ideas] helped me rethink my identity as a 'non-creative'...I am inherently creative and it manifests in ways I had never considered before, like improving processes, cooking, & parenting."

- Luke, Manufacturing Company Owner

"These concepts helped me lean into expressions that make my heart come alive and affectionately hold close things that bring joy once again, after experiencing great pain and loss."

- Kendra, Nurse

"Creativity Unlocked is a powerful, beautiful book. I have worked in the creative industries for over a decade, performed for over 100,000 people around the world, and created videos for top artists and labels, and I still found within it a wealth of wisdom, encouragement, and practical tools. Reading it with my wife, who loves her creativity, was a great way to connect and share more about who we are. I would highly recommend it!"

- Graham, Creative Director

"I've loved considering how I can use creativity to problem-solve and add joy to things that feel mundane, like folding laundry. It helped me remember passions that I had forgotten, and discover what makes me unique."

- Megan, Holistic Health Professional

"*Creativity Activated* is the perfect tool to help bring focus to a sometimes messy inward process. The content guides you through translating what's inside into outward expressions of creativity, growth, and forward movement that increase joy."

- Amanda, Teacher

"[The Creativity Unlocked Workshop] revealed to me that I use creativity in all areas of my life... I had forgotten how to use creativity outside of my writing, drawing and sewing..."

- Debra, Entrepreneur

"*Creativity Activated* helped me start writing for the first time in a decade. I found myself coming up with creative solutions for my art and other parts of life, too. It was healing to find out that this creativity was just dormant, not gone, and now coming back to life."

- Annette, Mother and Dreamer

DEDICATION

To my parents and loved ones, and to past, present, and future generations.
Thank you for making dreams come true.

TABLE OF CONTENTS

ABOUT THIS WORKBOOK

Welcome to *Creativity Activated*! Over the past few years, the science-informed concepts and heart-shaping exercises in this workbook have helped engineers, consultants, medical professionals, artists, academics and more rediscover and upgrade their creative process. Through these tools, individuals have found clarity for their careers, birthed art and initiatives into the world, discovered new income streams, deepened meaningful friendships, increased the delight and satisfaction in daily routines, and rewritten the stories of their lives.

Creative thought releases joy chemicals in the brain but many people are learning how to experience more of this natural benefit. No matter how experienced you are, there is always opportunity to increase the meaning and delight you find in what you are creating. Whether you are looking to get unstuck in a specific project, find fresh purpose in your work, improve problem-solving and ideation, strengthen relationships or community, or try something for the very first time, this workbook can help. Your creative outputs flows from what is happening within you. This resource is designed to help you increase joy and purpose by exploring and strengthening the connection between your internal world and your external experiences of expressions in your work, hobbies, and home life.

Creativity Activated can serve as a companion resource for the book *Creativity Unlocked* or as a standalone tool. It is designed to provide space for reflection and an array of practical exercises that will help you apply the concepts. Each new section starts with a review of the most important ideas from a chapter in *Creativity Unlocked*. Even if you are already familiar with this content, it can be helpful to revisit the concepts before diving into the exercises and reflection questions. However, if you find yourself getting stuck in the summaries, feel free to skip ahead. The goal is to have experiences of joy and connection in your creativity, not to fill out every box or line. Note: this workbook does not include all of the illustrative stories of people creating through a range of professions and experiences that are found in *Creativity Unlocked*. However, it does include an abundance of exercises and additional personal reflections not found in the book.

INTRODUCTION
How to get the most from Creativity Activated

Whether you are confident or inexperienced in recognizing your creative nature, there are new wells of joy and flow to discover. I am excited for the discoveries you will make, the projects and products you will develop, the art that you will release into the world. But what I desire most is that this tool would help you fall in love with your creative nature, and yourself, all over again.

If I could wave a stick over your head or had a machine that could laser off the limitations robbing your creativity, I would use it. But the creative growth process doesn't work that way. Instead, it mirrors the journey of human development. In order to grow both as humans and in our creativity, we must consume nutrients, engage with new ideas, move out of old stages or understandings, put concepts into practice, go on adventures big and small, and be part of relationships that encourage and see us through difficulty.

Throughout this workbook, we will look at science, reflect on the mindsets and beliefs shaping our stories, activate and practice our expressions, and talk a lot about meaningful connection—a concept that fuels creativity and that many sources indicate is associated with having a fulfilled, fruitful life. You'll discover simple techniques for your daily activities and learn from the findings of scientists who study the creative ability of thought to spark new experiences via the brain. Many of the practical keys and activating tools draw from the field of psychology.

Even though there is work ahead, I have good news for you: this journey can be full of surprising amounts of joy and satisfaction. You can think of this workbook as a collection of keys. There are ones that are sleek and light and others that are weightier because they work on different locks. Some will open the proverbial doors around you right now and provide clarity for present barriers and next steps. Others you are adding to your keyring in preparation for future seasons. All will help unlock insights into what makes you tick and what fuels your fire as a creative being.

So, why wait? Discover the space decorator, rhyme spitter, business leader, overseas adventurer, romantic poet, or social impact activist within you. There are passions and creative roles waiting to be recognized and joyfully activated. Get ready to uncover more of the treasure that you carry and every day ways that you can release beauty and goodness into the world. Your expressions represent a unique sound in the world that is meant to be heard, whether by one person or a multitude. Along the way of discovering new outputs, you can learn practical strategies for enhancing how you enjoy, complete, and share creative expressions. It's not too late, even if you feel like you are at square one. Now is the perfect moment to start creating something new in your story. If you get stuck, don't worry. Pause or skip to another section, and come back when you are ready. Take your journey one step at a time.

Happy creating,
Chris

Chapter 1
CREATIVITY

You. Are. Creative. It's time to recognize how your creativity is present and powerful in different parts of life. Tap into fresh joy and meaning by intentionally creating throughout your weekly routine.

KEY CONCEPTS
Creativity Unlocked – Chapter 1

The Case for Creativity

Creativity is transformative. It turns materials, places, situations, and even challenges into something new. It's the gift of creativity that solves problems around the house and develops technology and solutions that transform the world. Today, you will use multiple devices and items, including this workbook, which were the outflows of others' creative journeys. Properly activated, your creative nature can spark delight and add meaning to life in the midst of the uncertainty of a rapidly changing world. When we build, make, design, speak, share, praise, elevate, or refine something in a way that simply makes us smile, it satisfies a part of us that is hard to quantify. According to researchers at Drexel University, creative cognition activates joy chemicals in the brain.* Yes, the world needs the problem-solving power of your creativity, but you need it first: for the delight and purpose it can enable.

Maybe you don't think this workbook is for you because you're "not creative"? You're not alone. In a recent study by Adobe, only 41 percent of respondents worldwide described themselves as creative.** This is an all-too-common belief that is robbing the world of joy and problem-solving power. Many have learned definitions that clumsily confuse creativity with artistic talent. Creativity is a quality in every person that goes far beyond the ability to paint, draw, or sing well. The first definition in the Merriam-Webster Dictionary's definition for create is "to bring into existence." We will be using this broad definition throughout this curriculum.

You do not need to be a photographer, vocalist, or sculptor to be creative! And if you enjoy activating creativity via art, this quality extends far beyond your craft or techniques! Researchers Michele and Robert Root-Bernstein, authors of Sparks of Genius, also affirm this wider view, writing: "It's too bad that when considering what endeavors may be creative, people immediately think of the arts. It's the problem-solving processes they exhibit rather than the content or craft that make them so. Just about anything we do can be addressed in a creative manner, from housecleaning to personal hobbies to work."***

Sure, your childhood crayon drawings were creative, but so is making lunch for a friend, going back to school for a new career, solving a crossword puzzle, mentoring youth in your community, walking in a city park, even reading these words. Every day, people are creating: raising families, accomplishing tasks at work, navigating relationships, planning trips, engaging in experiences or other hobbies, solving problems, and more. If you are someone who enjoys art, a broader definition of creativity can help fuel your expressions and connect them to different parts of life. And if recognizing your creativity is difficult, activating this quality can benefit your career, hobbies, and relationships.

*Source: Yongtaek Oh, Christine Chesebrough, Brian Erickson, Fengqing Zhang, and John Kounios (2020), "An Insight-Related Neural Reward Signal," NeuroImage 214 (116757): 116757. https://doi. org/10.1016/j.neuroimage.2020.116757.
**Source: Adobe, State of Create, accessed September 2021, https://www. adobe.com/content/dam/acom/en/max/pdfs/AdobeStateofCreate_2016_Report_Final.pdf.
***Source: Robert and Michele Root-Bernstein, Sparks of Genius (Boston: Houghton Mifflin, 1999).

Experts on the human brain embrace a broader definition of creativity that starts with what is happening in our heads. According to cognitive scientist Art Markman, "Every day, we use language to speak sentences that have never been spoken... [we] express thoughts that have never been expressed. All of this is so deeply ingrained that we don't notice how creative it is."*

Aligning Creative Expressions With Goals and Passion

The question is not if you are creating, but what and how you are creating, and whether you are benefitting from the process. Many of us don't consistently take time to explore whether what we're expressing and producing is in alignment with our goals and needs. Or we haven't had a process that effectively unlocks the joy and purpose that creativity can hold. Here are a few eclectic examples of creativity in daily settings:

- An elementary school teacher works with a family to develop a learning plan
- A service representative identifies steps to resolve a customer's situation
- A consultant refines a PowerPoint deck to more clearly communicate data
- A shopper figures out the most time-efficient path at a grocery store
- A painter mixes oils into different colors and builds a new easel

Creativity holds keys for personal growth. When facing a short-term obstacle or long-term problem, we need to be able to diagnose what is wrong and identify tools or practices that can bring a solution. But we also require something beyond analysis: the motivation, the energy, and the perseverance to implement the needed changes. We can know the answers but still struggle to implement them, especially when a challenge gets scary or hard. Where do we find the missing motivation to move forward? What we need in the moment is hope, which is more than a transient feeling or a cheesy slogan. It's the expectation of future good that motivates us to take our next step forward. When we can find joy or satisfaction in our creativity, we can have a present experience of goodness that naturally fuels this positivity for the future.

All of us go through hard times, and none of us have arrived as fully developed human beings. If you have, you can stop reading now and go eat some ice cream. For the rest of us, the music we make, the subjects we're learning, the family we love, or the hobbies we enjoy can help us keep showing up in difficult seasons. However, we can all too easily de-prioritize our expressions when facing challenges. Or we feel unworthy of the creative goodness that sparks hope and motivates persistence. It is in these moments where we most need to have fun, satisfying routines for our expressions that can help us process difficulties and persevere through hard times. We can build joy capital: stockpiles of experiences of delight and meaningful connection activated through our creativity. Then, when adversity arises, our perception and ability to respond are vastly different. Problems look more like blips on a map full of meaningful creativity versus the latest addition to a landscape overwhelmed by difficulty.

Our interests may be different, our passions unique, our stories a world apart, but what we do have in common is our innate creative nature. Whether you express yourself through sock drawers, sonnets, snow machines, soup recipes, or spreadsheets, you are creative. There are opportunities closer than you think, small and big, to add joy and purpose to your daily routine.

*Source: Arthur B. Markman and Kristin L. Wood, Tools for Innovation: The Science behind the Practical Methods That Drive New Ideas, (New York: Oxford Press, 2009).

JOURNAL PROMPT
Creativity Unlocked – Chapter 1

RECOGNIZE YOUR CREATIVITY

Creativity is present in every part of our lives. Even in settings where we lack full vision, ownership, or control, we are still bringing something into existence, whether a moment, an experience, a conversation, a solution, or something else. The first step toward greater activation of creativity is awareness. Here are a few examples of how varied creative expression can be:

- *Hobbies & Free Time*
    - Listening to a podcast or radio show
    - Completing a group workout class
    - Exploring a new artistic hobby like pottery or poetry
- *Work or School*
    - Having lunch with a colleague or classmate
    - Solving a calculation problem
    - Developing a strategic plan for your team
- *Family and Relationships*
    - Going on a walk in the park with a family member
    - Picking out new furniture with a loved one
    - Hosting a holiday gathering

Now it's your turn. Use the space below to write out ways that you're creating in different parts of your life, like the examples above. Try to list at least three expressions for each category. The purpose is to get the juices flowing around recognizing your creativity, which is the first step toward more joy-filled experiences. Want a challenge? Grab a blank sheet of paper and see how many total expressions you can identify.

1) Hobbies & Free Time

2) Work or School

3) Family and Relationships

ACTIVATION EXERCISE
Creativity Unlocked – Chapter 1

SEE DAILY TASKS ANEW

Choose one place or environment from the previous activity. It might be your workplace, your home, your favorite park, your rock climbing gym, or somewhere else. Brainstorm some new ways to create or express yourself within that context.

Stumped on how to do this? Here are some examples. Use these as inspiration to write out your own, the more specific the better.

☐ Write a note of genuine appreciation for a colleague or family member.

☐ Prepare a themed meal or a new dish, complete with decorations, for someone special in your life.

☐ Mix up your exercise routine at the gym/studio. Google ideas if needed.

☐ Spend fifteen minutes brainstorming a new story, organization, or trip.

☐ Try a new routine or different commute for work. Use a different scheduling system or see how many people you can make smile.

☐ _____

☐ _____

☐ _____

☐ _____

Well done! Now it's time to activate creativity in a new way. **Pick one idea from your list that feels lighthearted or that brings you excitement and complete it.**

When you're done, take a few minutes to reflect on the experience. Answer the questions below and make sure to celebrate the creative steps you have taken.

How did intentionally creating via the activity you picked make you feel?

What was most enjoyable about the process? What was difficult?

What other ideas do you have for intentional creativity in your daily life?

Is there anything else that you would like to note for your ongoing creative exploration? Write out questions or sparks of inspiration here.

KEY COLLECTION ZONE

What ideas resonated with you most from this section? Use this space to make a note after your first reading and leave space to return and add keys you find as you continue your journey. These could be words to remember, ideas to revisit, or practical steps to take that apply these concepts.

CREATIVITY KEY

CREATIVITY KEY

CREATIVITY KEY

 ## CREATIVITY GUIDE CORNER – Let Go and Let Flow
Personal reflections to consider. Follow @one.step.growth on social media for more.

For decades I believed the lie that I wasn't creative. I didn't understand how much this gift could benefit my life. My understanding limited this quality only to the arts and to individuals that had expressions validated by others. Shortly after finishing my MBA at Harvard I reached a low point via a struggle with alcohol that sparked a search for clarity and hope. It also provided the opportunity to examine how I processed thoughts and feelings. When I returned to a corporate tech job with a new approach fueled by concepts in this workbook, I began to see how different parts of life could combine in joyful ways. Courage to take on new creative projects grew as I found meaningful expressions in work, daily routines, and art.

The threads of creative expression can weave together in unexpected ways. I had no idea that I would make electronic music, start a nonprofit to capture hope-filled stories of addiction recovery, move unexpectedly to a small city, produce a documentary, or write a book and develop tools that help others rediscover joy-filled creativity in their own lives. I also didn't anticipate how much joy and purpose these expressions would bring. Small experiments fueled delight and connection that inspired more exploration. Where you end up may surprise you. This workbook's keys will be an aid in overcoming barriers. They can also help you build an approach to taking healthy creative risks throughout your life, aligned with your interests and capacity. Tasting the benefits of creating will fuel capacity for growth.

Chapter 2
MINDSETS

Changing the lenses through which you see your expressions and yourself can empower totally different experiences of your creativity. Use simple tools to activate a fresh perspective and spark exploration.

KEY CONCEPTS
Creativity Unlocked – Chapter 2

The Power and Potential of Lenses

Your mindsets are lenses that shape how you see yourself and your creativity. Like a camera or a social media filter, they can magnify or shrink, dim or heighten, color or shadow wondrous details. When they are clarified, or distorted, what is in front of you appears differently. Have you ever witnessed someone have a response to an event or piece of news completely different from your own? They likely have a different lens informing their reaction that they have either naturally adopted or intentionally learned. Your creativity actually starts with your internal reality. Thoughts and words are expressions you release into the world that bring something new into existence for yourself or others and that continue to shape your mindsets. For better or worse, they will continue to color how you experience creativity.

I have good news for you: the lenses through which you see can shift. Upgrading your mindsets can unlock ease and joy in your creative process. Your brain is neuroplastic, meaning that it is continually changing. "Habits of thinking need not be forever. One of the most significant findings of psychology in the past twenty years is that individuals choose the way they think," states Dr. Martin Seligman, pioneer of positive psychology and author of *Learned Optimism: How to Change Your Mind and Life.** Neuroscientist Dr. Caroline Leaf explains in her book, *Switch on Your Brain*, that, "Thoughts are real, physical things that occupy mental real estate. Moment by moment, every day, you are changing the structure of your brain through your thinking. When we hope, it is an activity of the mind that changes the structure of our brain."**

Shame: the Creativity Killer

Mindsets tinged with shame, or feeling "not enough," are a common reason for creativity to feel blocked or unpleasant. Shame is a toxic ingredient that poisons one's internal reality and creative process. It fuels the impostor syndrome and fears that can either paralyze or keep one in a frenzied state of creating to prove one's value or worth. These pressures are exhausting and can rob joy and inspiration from expression. Shifting these mindsets can unlock creativity.

You don't have to work exhaustingly to prove your value. Your creative outflows do not define, determine, or justify your worth or significance; they reveal that it's already there. Your humanity makes you innately valuable. Intentional practices can help build new mindsets that provides a foundation of love and self-worth for your expressions. There are a range of steps that can help you kick shame in the face: (1) recognizing its influence, (2) embracing a new thought instead of an old one, (3) connecting with community, (4) practicing self-compassion, (5) addressing trigger points, and (6) experiencing joy-filled creativity that reinforces new, positive mindsets. Shifting mindsets is not about denying or stuffing down feelings; that won't help. Rather, it's exploring and choosing a new thought that offers a different perspective about yourself and your creativity. Sooner or later, your feelings will shift, too.

*Source: Martin E. P. Seligman, Learned Optimism: How to Change Your Mind and Your Life (New York: Vintage Books, 2006).
**Source: Caroline Leaf, Switch on Your Brain (Grand Rapids, MI: Baker Books, 2013).

JOURNAL PROMPT
Creativity Unlocked – Chapter 2

CHANGING YOUR LENSES

Your natural state is to create. Where are you wanting to experience more momentum, joy, or clarity in your creativity? Writing and speaking out positive affirmations about yourself and your creativity can help upgrade your mindsets. Your thoughts and words help shape the lenses that impact your experiences, especially when paired with aligned experiences. To start, list out expressions where you feel stuck or specific thought patterns that are hindering your process.

Example: *I feel like my writing isn't good enough; I'm not creative; parenting; finishing projects, math.*

Expression:

Expression:

Expression:

Now it's to time develop personalized affirmations that can help align your thoughts and words with the values and perspectives you aspire to have. It's a part of rewiring the neural pathways in your brain. You can incorporate guidance on the attributes of effective affirmations drawn from the book *The Success Principle* by Jack Canfield. Not every affirmation has to follow all these rules, but they're a good starting point.

- Use "I am..." statements
- Use positive statement—the word "no" or "not" does not appear in the statement
- State goal or desire as if it's already achieved or reality
- State specific positive affirmations about yourself and creativity in the present tense
- Use brief and memorable wording
- Focus language on yourself, and not other people
- Use specific action words

Your affirmations don't have to be long, eloquent, or complicated. The first goal is to make sure they are both authentic and hope-filled. They are meant to be aspirational, but also not so far-fetched they seem unbelievable. Instead of "I am a billionaire NBA star," something like "I celebrate my passion for creating via sports" or "I am learning to steward financial resources" will be more impactful. Try to find at least one for each idea that you listed above. Refine until you find language that resonates or that appropriately counters the negativity you've felt.

JOURNAL PROMPT
Creativity Unlocked – Chapter 2

CHANGING YOUR LENSES

Here are a few examples of effective affirmations that you can incorporate or rephrase for your own:

- I am creative; I am a problem-solver; I have a unique story
- I am willing to embrace new belief systems about myself and my creativity that bring hope and joy; if I love what I create, that's enough
- I choose to find enjoyment and beauty in every creative process
- I am the type of person that inspiration flows through
- My creative future is better than I think and beyond what my past has held
- I can come alive and find delight in my creative expressions
- I have permission to explore and experiment with creativity, regardless of whether my efforts leads to something seen or rewarded by others
- I am a writer who cheerfully creates worlds with words
- I create a positive atmosphere in my workplace
- I am a loving parent who celebrates the expression and creativity of my children

Grab a pen and use the lines below to write out affirmations for your creative process.

1. _____
2. _____
3. _____
4. _____
5. _____
6. _____
7. _____

ACTIVATION EXERCISE
Creativity Unlocked – Chapter 2

USE YOUR VOICE

Now, take five minutes to say your positive affirmations out loud. If you're in a public place, this might be a little awkward, but perhaps you could go to the restroom, sit in your car for a few minutes, or wait until you're at home. Without getting too far into the neurological explanation, know that it can be helpful to say the affirmations out loud.

Let's start with three statements we have provided, and then continue with the personalized affirmations that you created in the journaling exercise. Take a deep breath. As you exhale, release any pressure you feel. As you inhale, focus on the opportunity and hope that this journey represents.

- **I am creative.** My creativity is valuable regardless of the fruit I have or lack right now. My creativity is a part of me that I will never lose and is just as important as that of others around me. I choose to look with new eyes at creativity in my life.

- **My creative voice and expressions are unique and multi-dimensional.** I recognize my creative nature through my work, relationships, experiences, problem-solving, and hobbies. I give myself permission to learn more about my creativity, and to grow in this area. I live free of the pressure to have it all together or to share my expressions with others.

- **I can partner with hope and love through my thoughts, words, and actions every day.** I recognize the opportunity I have to create through my thoughts, words, and actions. I choose to partner with love and hope as best I can, and give myself permission to be imperfect in the process.

Try incorporating this as a regular practice in your day for at least one week. Set a daily alarm or reminder on your phone so that you remember. You could also put your written list somewhere that you can easily review and read aloud, like on your bathroom mirror. As you continue to discover creative expressions in your life, you can come back and add specific affirmations for them here. Want to take it one step further? Develop a creative way to display these positive thoughts in your home. As you continue practicing affirmations, take note of practical situations or activities that you begin to experience differently.

KEY COLLECTION ZONE

What ideas resonated with you most from this section? Use this space to record after your first reading and leave space to return and add keys you find as you continue your journey. These could be words to remember, ideas to revisit, or practical steps to take that apply these concepts.

CREATIVITY KEY

CREATIVITY KEY

CREATIVITY KEY

 **CREATIVITY GUIDE CORNER – The Power of Inside-Out**
Personal reflections to consider. Follow @one.step.growth on social media for more.

It's possible to have lots of opportunities and resources but lack the internal thought processes that enable joy and momentum in creativity. My education and financial security did not prevent me from feeling stuck in life or becoming addicted and hopeless. Knowledge, skills, and resources can flavor and empower what you create in the world but they don't guarantee a life-giving approach. I was skeptical of some ideas I considered "pop psychology" until I began to experience how impactful they could be. Rewiring my brain played a significant role in upgrading creativity, and there's research to support this approach.

Intentional mindsets work changed how I saw myself and my expressions, which altered how I showed up in creative moments. These shifts helped spark opportunities in songwriting, relationships, and my career, around which I previously was more passive. For a lot of my life, I lived as if changing my external circumstances or simply achieving more could address insecurity and relieve the pressure that clouded my mind. I kept showing up in ways less than who I actually was or how I could create. Practical situations affect creativity, but what I needed most was a shift to an inside-out approach. Instead of waiting for external circumstances or credentials to change, I started using internal transformation tools found in this section. The ease and joy of creativity increased. While other people played key parts in the process, I still had to do the work to learn over time to see myself through new lenses.

Chapter 3
EXPRESSION

Where is pressure robbing you of joy and freedom in your creativity? Get ready to ditch the limitations and express yourself in work, art, hobbies, or home life in ways that bring you satisfaction. If you enjoy it, that's enough.

KEY CONCEPTS
Creativity Unlocked – Chapter 3

Quieting External Factors to Increase Internal Delight

A key aspect of unlocking joy and purpose in creativity is finding what brings personal satisfaction, whether or not anyone offers praise or a reward. My hope is that you discover creative expressions that make you stop and stare, that you crave like I crave In'n'Out burgers. Experiencing this personal satisfaction increases freedom and joy in the process of creating, and not just the outcome. This can spark new ideas, greater motivation, and the refreshing benefits of creativity. Research has shown that this naturally-occurring "intrinsic" motivation is associated with higher satisfaction, longevity, and performance in work settings. This internal resonance helps us navigate external pressures, avoid distraction, quiet criticism, and more.

Many of us have missed out on the potential delight and power of creativity because we have focused too much on rewards or validation from others. We over-prioritize "likes" on social media or payment from someone for our expression and miss out on personal meaning and joy it can bring. Or, we have not had time or felt permission to find and celebrate outflows that truly resonate with us. In *Creativity Unlocked* and this workbook, we take an approach emphasizing "creative themes" to show there are many ways to express one's passions and interests. Themes are topics, specific activities, or skills, like jazz history, organizing spaces, or welding, that can be activated in multiple ways. One could write about or start a business related to these interests or listen to Louis Armstrong while cleaning house or fixing a car. Quieting external pressures and activating expressions that spark personal delight is a big part of reclaiming fun and ease in creativity. In a world where checking the boxes and pleasing others is emphasized, it's crucial to make space for finding and growing this internal resonance.

Let's dive deeper into the difference between external and intrinsic motivators. The former are received from others: reward, compensation, attention, validation, feedback, recognition. The latter are naturally experienced or felt regardless of the outcome, like joy, satisfaction, excellence, meaning, wonder, or curiosity. External motivators are not bad; they play an important role in our growth and life. Input from friends, customer feedback, income, advice from mentors, and even correction are important parts of flourishing. But external validators can be easily over-prioritized in a society where everything seems to be measured: return on investment, followers, engagement, profit, impact. This workbook is an opportunity to revisit how you prioritize external and internal motivators for what you are creating.

There are many wonderful and necessary activities that you may not have passion or joy for directly, but that bring meaning and satisfaction due to the connection they have with your values or with people you care about. Or, they enable you to fulfill a responsibility in your community or bring an important external reward. For instance, washing the dishes or running errands are not typically heart-alive experiences, but they support and strengthen healthy relationships and households, which bring longer-term joy and fulfillment. Recognizing aspects of one's creative role at work or in family can deepen intrinsic motivation for routine parts of life. You can also explore adding intrinsic joy expressions to your regular responsibilities, like making a game around cleaning or using a commute to indulge in a favorite podcast.

Branching Into Multiple Creative Passions

Picture your creativity like a tree. The branches heading in different directions are your expressions. The trunk and root system consist of your values, self-image, and mindsets. Support from others is the sunlight that helps growth, and the joy and meaningful connection found in creativity are the water that nourishes day in and day out. Some branches will naturally extend and develop. Other expressions may not grow as strong or bear fruit. But they're all still important for the tree's shape. Not all creative branches have to be productive to be of value. In fact, the permission to pursue expressions that don't have quantifiable impact, and the freedom from the need for fruitfulness, can accelerate authentic, inspiring creativity.

What is the stencil that you have felt pressure to fill via your expressions, whether in work, family, hobbies, or other settings? Many of us have tried to force ourselves and our creativity into someone else's design, and we've become frustrated, or worse. We end up lopping off interests that bring us joy but seem unimportant to others. Or we glue on branches that we feel like we're supposed to have, instead of allowing natural growth or a healthy grafting process. Granted, there can be great value and fruitfulness in learning from the creativity of others. Not all structures of tree growth are as beneficial or fruitful; there can be good reasons to intentionally shape or prune your creative tree. But, if you find yourself lacking passion or joy in your expressions, check to see if you're trying to fill the wrong shape. Heck, you might be a whole different species. A pear tree is going to have a hard time becoming a sequoia.

"People move from grade school to college to the workplace and are trained to focus on external motivators," shares Meredith Neumann, a licensed therapist and entrepreneur. After ten years in private practice, she started Scaling Within, a company that helps other entrepreneurs and business leaders strengthen their internal capacity and sustain external growth in their professional lives. "[They] often underestimate their own creative potential because of this overemphasis on an external locus of control that feels out of their hands. Rediscovering intrinsic motivation can open up whole new avenues and possibilities in the workplace, in hobbies, and in one's personal life."

Are there themes where you haven't felt permission to explore? It's time to dive in and create space to discover more activities, skills, and contexts that bring life to your heart. As you use the Resonance Map on the next few pages to identify themes, take note of places where there is a spark of interest or excitement but also resistance, questions, or fear. The barriers may indicate that something valuable lies on the other side. What is most precious for us often is the most vulnerable. You can take it one step at a time. This process is about trial and layer, not trial and error. You're not in search of one end-all, be-all solution. Take out the "right" and "wrong" thinking from your vocabulary around creativity; there is much to be discovered in nuance. If you find something that doesn't resonate as much, that's helpful learning. You may also just need to explore a slightly different application of theme, like pencils instead of paint.

JOURNAL PROMPT
Creativity Unlocked – Chapter 3
EXPLORING PERSONAL JOY & SATISFACTION

The brainstorming questions below are designed to help you identify activities, interests, and skills that bring a natural reward of joy or satisfaction. Take 15 - 20 minutes to journal out answers and try not to analyze or filter your responses. They don't have to be practical or make sense; this is a space for exploration and dreaming. Follow the flow into unexpected ideas.

1. What experiences, places, creative influences or memories make your heart come alive? Make a list. Where have you had those skin-tingling, I-can't-believe-I-get-to-do-this, deeply fulfilling moments? What activities make you lose track of time? These can be experiences that happened through your own creative expression, or through somebody else's.

2. What expressions or activities would you enjoy even if no one ever saw or knew the outcome? What hobbies, memories, or places bring you so much joy that you feel no need for recognition or sharing of them? What do you not need compensation or recognition to enjoy doing?

JOURNAL PROMPT
Creativity Unlocked – Chapter 3

EXPLORING PERSONAL JOY & SATISFACTION

3. How would you spend your time if you had all the money in the world? Think about how you would structure your life, and what dreams you would pursue. Helping others? Being the parent at every one of your kids' sports games? Working on a novel? Showing others beautiful parts of your neighborhood or distant places? Taking people on rejuvenating nature adventures? Building a company producing a world-changing product? Dare to dream about what could be without any pressure for a tangible, practical, or financial outcome.

JOURNAL PROMPT
Creativity Unlocked – Chapter 3

EXPLORING PERSONAL JOY & SATISFACTION

4. What brought you joy as a child? Before you learned what attracted validation or reward from others, what did you like to do? What were you drawn to or dreaming about? These early-in-life moments can indicate areas of passion undiluted by the pressure to please others or conform to surroundings. If your childhood did not offer opportunity for this exploration or play, think about a season in your adult life that felt the most light, carefree, or even silly.

5. What experiences do you believe you're supposed to enjoy, but you actually don't? Are there hobbies, activities, or aspects of culture in which you participate because it seems to be what a certain type of person is supposed to do? Where does your life feel more like performance or checking a box than true enjoyment? Do you create or hold back from certain tones, channels, or styles because of what others might do or think?

ACTIVATION EXERCISE
Creativity Unlocked – Chapter 3

BUILDING YOUR RESONANCE MAP

The questions above are the first step toward building your Resonance Map, which is a core component of the *Creativity Unlocked* approach. This tool is designed to be a living document that helps you find meaningful, heart-alive expressions via both daily creativity and longer-term projects. In short, it is a place where you can note activities, settings, or experiences in which you find intrinsic joy or delight. It will evolve over time. Here are the steps involved with developing your Resonance Map, some of which you have already started:

1. Pick your tool. You can use this workbook or pick a device or journal where you can record your thoughts and ideas and that you know you can access consistently. It could be a notebook, a Google doc, an iPhone app, a planner, a vision board, or something else.

2. Mark out three sections. The first part is for brainstorming ideas and capturing experiences in a less-structured way; you just completed this section via the questions above. The second step is to explore the patterns in your answers above and look for themes that appear via your reflections. You'll do this next. The third section is for mapping out areas for application in your life. Our diagram divides the final section into applications for personal life, professional life, and everything else, but you might find it better to create more specific categories. Make sure to include parts of life that feel more difficult in which to identify creative expression.

3. Continue inputting resonant ideas, activities, and topics. More ideas will arise and clarity will grow as you have experiences of activities, people, places, and skills that help you feel joy, meaning, or more-fully alive in creativity -- or the opposite. Anything can be helpful inputs, from songs to movie quotes to inventions to historical events to scents. Along with what sparks joy, you might also want to have a separate space to note what frustrates you. These areas can indicate challenges and possible solutions that would bring you great satisfaction to create around. When you're starting, set a regular time to repeat brainstorming, reflection on themes, and application. New ideas will arise. The following pages contain helpful examples.

4. Identify creative themes and ways to activate them. Reflect on the data points that you have gathered and look for patterns or similarities across your answers. Remember: themes can be topics and interests, skillsets and qualities, or specific activities around which you create. Clarity and variety will increase as you continue exploring. Once you have several themes identified, brainstorm ways to apply them for both current and future seasons of life. For instance, you could bring a theme of visual design into a work presentation, refresh with a podcast on this subject during your commute, or pursue training. If you enjoy cooking and deep conversations, you could start a dinner or book club that combines these themes.

ACTIVATION EXERCISE
Creativity Unlocked – Chapter 3

THE RESONANCE MAP: LIVING RECORD

Find a place where you can note and return to moments, activities, dreams, experiences, and other things that have brought you joy.

NOTES APP

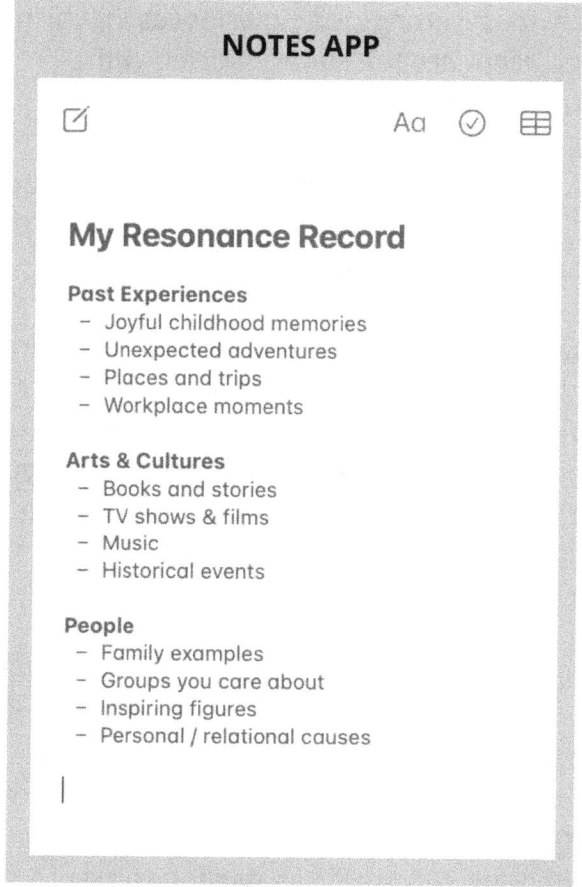

JOURNAL

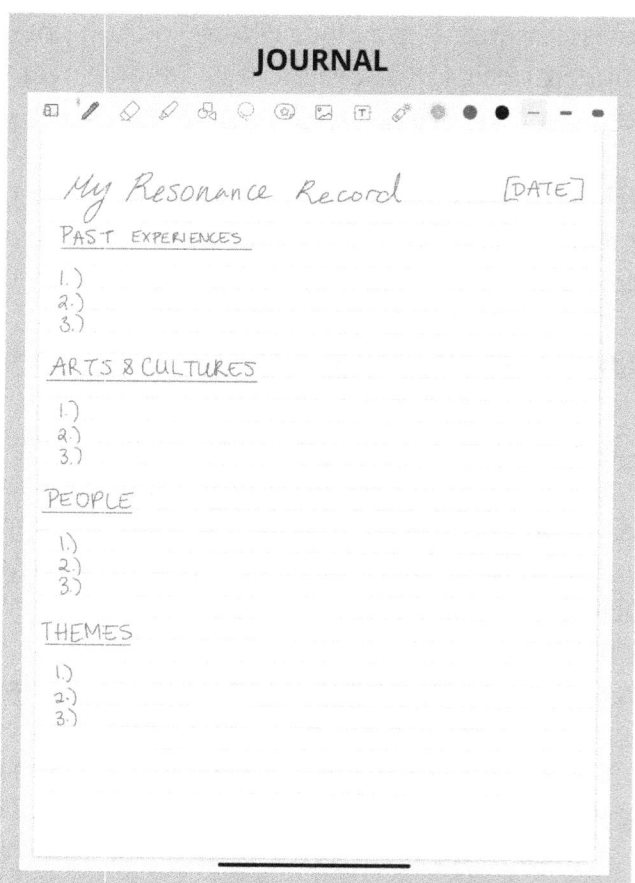

SPREADSHEET

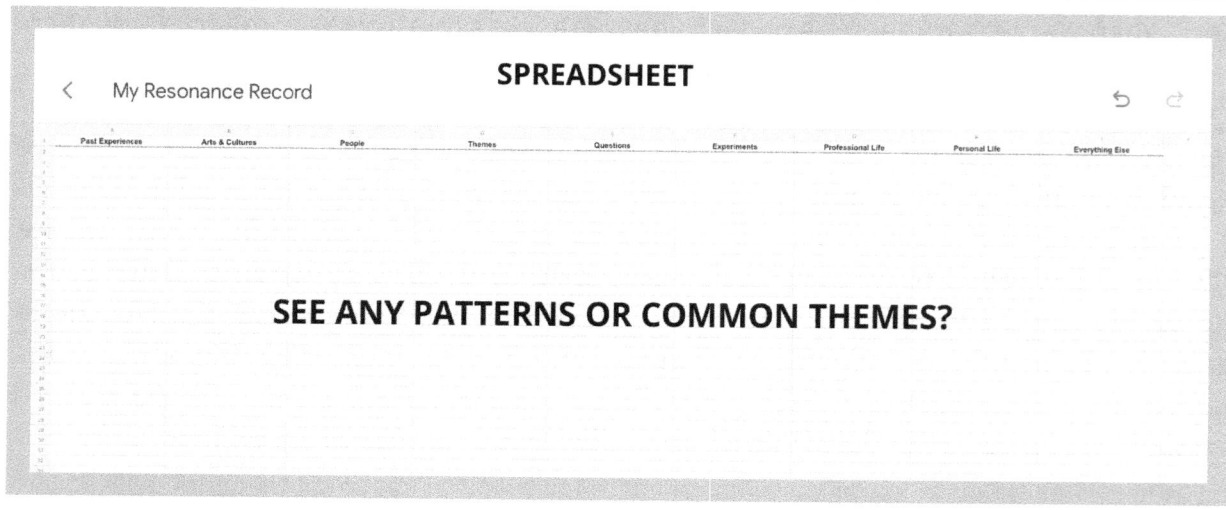

SEE ANY PATTERNS OR COMMON THEMES?

ACTIVATION EXERCISE
Creativity Unlocked – Chapter 3

HOW TO IDENTIFY THEMES FOR YOUR RESONANCE MAP

Look through your reflections to the questions above. Can you spot patterns or similarities across different experiences? It's alright to get imaginative and stretch the boundaries. Playing with Lego could indicate a theme around working with your hands, medieval architecture, or interior design. Seeing these ideas and experiences as connected clues will help you flesh out and determine themes that you can try. Clarity and proof will grow as you experiment and find more creative joy in your work, hobbies, or home life. Some ways of activating a general theme might resonate more than others. For instance, within music you might enjoy songwriting but not producing beats, or the numbers of structural engineering but not accounting. The lists below are examples.

Abstract Qualities and Skills
Bringing order to chaos
Making new friends
Pushing yourself to the limits
Making processes more efficient
Pursuing harmony among different views
Breaking new ground
Doing in-depth study
Helping people achieve their goals
Brainstorming new ideas
Competing for a prize
Solving problems
Developing clever phrases
Structuring information for clarity

Topics and Interests
Cybersecurity
Clothing and accessories
Racial justice
Computer literacy
Jazz music
Eighteenth-century philosophers
Neuroscience
Reality television
Latin dance
Marine biology
Mental health and wellbeing
Food presentation
Architecture

Activities
Planning team gatherings
Practicing meditation and spiritual practices
Creating colorful art
Analyzing revenue channels
Fixing a vehicle or machinery
Recycling used clothes
Developing training curriculum
Writing fiction novels
Collaborating with a close friend on a project
Teaching kids your favorite game
Running outdoors
Playing the trumpet
Rock climbing or other adventure sports

ACTIVATION EXERCISE
Creativity Unlocked – Chapter 3

HOW TO IDENTIFY THEMES FOR YOUR RESONANCE MAP

How is your theme identification process going? If you need ideas, ask a friend or seek input from someone you trust. Or, check out onestepgrowth.com for workshops, groups, and other resources that could be helpful. Once you've identified recurring themes for your journey, add them to the boxes in the image below. Like a tree, your creativity has multiple branches. **Remember: you can always update your creative themes as your journey continues.**

ACTIVATION EXERCISE
Creativity Unlocked – Chapter 3

RESONANCE MAP: APPLICATION

Use the spaces below to brainstorm opportunities for activating themes in different aspects of your life. There are more opportunities than you might think. though you might need help from others to see them. Clarity and confidence will increase as you test and learn over time.

THEME	
Family Life	
Work Life	
Service	
Free Time	
Other	

ACTIVATION EXERCISE
Creativity Unlocked – Chapter 3

15 MINUTE CREATIVITY SPARK

It's time to get out of your comfy reading chair and put this chapter into practice. Set a timer for fifteen minutes, and start creating. You can take the practical steps you've brainstormed about in the journaling exercise, or pick a different creative activity. Remember that it doesn't have to be artistic in nature. Start simple. For example, you could spend 15 minutes researching your next camping adventure, writing out the guest list for your next event, doodling with markers, writing an encouraging note to a friend, or rearranging the furniture in the living room.

Once you start, don't stop. Don't judge yourself in the process. At the end of the fifteen minutes, you can continue to create if you're finding a flow, or stop and try another activity.

Take time to repeat until you discover activities that connect for you, as your schedule allows. Sometimes trying various types of similar activities are necessary for finding your unique voice. For instance, you may dislike fifteen minutes of writing poetry, but discover joy in keeping a journal, developing a bulleted list of funny movie ideas, or writing a fake Wikipedia article for a character you want to create. Don't let your assumption of what it has to look like keep you from discovering your flow. You may find yourself connecting more or less with different aspects of activities and themes.

I recommend using this 15 Minute Creativity Spark whenever you notice you're overthinking your creative expression, when you haven't felt inspired for a while, or simply as a regular exercise to keep your creative outlets fresh and joy-focused. Reflect periodically on the new outflows you discover. Some may be infrequent or one-time expressions; others may become a central part of your life.

Make a plan for adding in regular time for creative experimentation to your schedule. Whether it's in shorter, more frequent time blocks or a quarter day once a month, practical experiences are crucial for enjoying and unlocking the benefits of your creativity. If you have trouble staying consistent, ask a friend to help with accountability. The more you experiment and explore, the easier it becomes. If the process feels uncomfortable at first, don't give up.

Write out a two sentence plan for regular creative activations that fits your schedule.

KEY COLLECTION ZONE

What ideas resonated with you most from this section? Use this space to record after your first reading and leave space to return and add keys you find as you continue your journey. These could be words to remember, ideas to revisit, or practical steps to take that apply these concepts.

CREATIVITY KEY

CREATIVITY KEY

CREATIVITY KEY

 **CREATIVITY GUIDE CORNER - Learning to Hear Your Heart**
Personal reflections to consider. Follow @one.step.growth on social media for more.

When I started exploring creativity, I was not used to listening to my heart. Throughout life, my decision making had revolved around whether others would validate or reward me. Letting go of these priorities got easier over time, but it took practice. Looking back, I can see linkages between my current creative expressions and heart-alive moments via middle school dance music, favorite podcasts and toys, and childhood career aspirations. For instance, recognizing my passion for electronic act Swedish House Mafia led to jotting down lyric ideas one night. This prepared me for an unexpected opportunity to co-write an EDM song that sparked incredible joy. Similarly, the meaning I find in addiction recovery and mental health fueled steps to strengthen my skillset and take new risks in storytelling.

Some of the most helpful discoveries I've made in the last few years of creative exploration are expressions or contexts that *don't* provide as much personal meaning or joy. We all have limited time and resources, so shifting capacity from what matters less to that which resonates deeply can be helpful. When I started, some expressions felt too vulnerable, too far-fetched, or too risky to pursue. You might feel the same. That's okay. Courage and capacity to experiment will grow as you taste the benefits. This is why trial and layer thinking is important: we can give ourselves permission to be in process of discovery and how to apply these themes in our lives in different seasons.

Chapter 4
PROCESS

The approach matters. It's possible to know what brings creative joy and still get bogged down or stuck in the process. Use science-informed keys to fuel fresh momentum and clarity for your expressions.

KEY CONCEPTS
Creativity Unlocked - Chapter 4

Embrace the Journey and Different Stages of Growth

When you have a moment, search for and watch a YouTube video of a baby giraffe. At times, exploring and activating your creativity will feel similar to its wobbly steps: brave, wonderful, and uncertain. You may experience a whole range of emotions: uncertainty, exhilaration, fear, wonder. The natural highs of expressions that bring intrinsic joy are incredible. But there also can be low points, where you feel frustrated, confused, or disappointed. Moments of perceived "success" or "failure" serve as an invitation to upgrading your growth process, both around specific outflows and how we engage with creativity more broadly.

It is important to learn to stay in touch with your needs: emotionally, physically, mentally, relationally, financially. The natural highs of creativity can sometimes paper over deficiencies in rest or opportunities to process emotional pain. The keys below are designed to help you navigate the ups and downs of the creative journey by building practices that help you steward your energy and capacity and protect your wellness. Remember: one of the most powerful ways we learn is when things go wrong. Here are eight keys for upgrading your process:

1. **Create achievable goals and practical plans.** Unrealistic expectations can torpedo your best efforts to create. Don't be afraid to start small. Remember, it's about baby steps.
2. **Give yourself permission to be imperfect.** If you're taking on an untried expression, or even trying a new approach to something you know, you're likely going to get it wrong at times. Things won't go as intended. Be kind to yourself; mess is part of the process.
3. **Embrace vulnerability and develop a plan for tough moments.** There will be times in your creative exploration that feel difficult or painful. Build a support system ahead of time.
4. **Find the hidden benefits of limitations.** Necessity can motivate invention. Fewer options offer clearer focus and a chance to exercise your creative mind. Start playing in the sandbox and get prepared for the opportunities that will bring you to the proverbial beach.
5. **Redefine success by celebrating every win.** Recognize steps or qualities you can praise; this fuels courage and momentum. Counter the inner critic with your words.
6. **Distinguish feelings from facts.** Emotions are temporary. When attempting something vulnerable, don't categorize or judge your efforts around creativity by immediate feelings.
7. **Express gratitude that proactively counters comparison.** When the voice of comparison starts to yap, take action to be thankful. Celebrate those who trigger insecurity.
8. **Follow the momentum.** When you tap into a creative flow, allow it to unfold. Find freedom and permission in the reminder that you create from worth, not for it.

Your creative journeys will likely contain advances and retreats. Mountaineers climbing the world's other highest peaks almost never venture from base camp to the top in one go. They advance up the mountain step-by-step, returning to camps as they acclimate. You are taking ground with every victory or learning opportunity that will benefit what you create in life.

JOURNAL PROMPT
Creativity Unlocked – Chapter 4

APPLYING KEYS TO YOUR PROCESS

Do you see opportunities to implement the concepts described above in your creative process? For this section's journaling activation, you're going to brainstorm ways that three or four keys from this chapter could benefit your process. Remember: we all are continually learning, so don't be overly negative toward yourself. Use the lines below or grab a piece of paper and list situations or areas where you need to implement these tips. Make a bullet-pointed list, or write it out free-form. If you get stuck, you can use these questions.

- For which expressions do you need more self-compassion and permission to explore?
- Where do you struggle with perfectionism or healthy goal-setting around creativity?
- Where do feelings or comparisons overwhelm you?
- Where have you felt stuck due to limited capacity, resources, skills, or opportunities?
- What examples of creative momentum have you experienced?

From these reflections, pick two or three challenges to your process that feel most important to tackle first. Along with taking practical steps, upgrading your mindsets around these areas is helpful. Write out a positive truth statement that will guide you going forward and add this to your affirmations list from the Mindsets section. For example, if one of your struggles is with comparison, your truth statement could be: "I choose to celebrate my unique expression every time I create." Remind yourself of this affirmation and repeat it out loud whenever you find yourself in a situation that triggers you into comparison. These sentences may be specific to certain expressions or serve as core values that guide your creativity over the long term. Once you have your list, put it in a place where you can revisit it. Let it remind and encourage you when you find yourself stuck or sliding back into negative thoughts.

ACTIVATION EXERCISE
Creativity Unlocked – Chapter 4

BABY GIRAFFE STEPS

For each key that you've journaled about, brainstorm a practical step that will help you implement the truth statement you've picked.

For example, if perfectionism is a struggle for you, think of a creative project you could do where you intentionally make a mess or make something weird, quirky, ugly, or imperfect. You can also start creating with the reminder that no one else has to see it. Your expression is worth exploring, regardless of the result. Lower the stakes and focus on the simple joy of creating.

If you wrestle with the belief that you don't have enough experience, knowledge or resources to create, start a project where you set extreme limits for yourself. Play a song with only four chords or notes, color or shade the images on the next page, write a poem with only half of the letters of the alphabet, cook a meal with only four ingredients, go on an outdoor adventure within five miles of your home, try to make a friend laugh without using any words, shop for a quirky item for your home or wardrobe with only a few dollars. The sky's the limit when it comes to creating within boundaries.

Write down one specific, practical step next to each key or area of challenge on your list. Then, pick one and go do it. Put this book away and have fun with it. Don't delay, because the longer you wait, the more likely it is that your area of challenge will convince you it's not necessary to do it. Jump into action, and don't forget you have permission to laugh your way through. These are your own wobbly baby giraffe steps.

1 _____

2 _____

3 _____

4 _____

BABY GIRAFFE STEPS: FREE COLOR SPACE

Bonus activity: use the coloring outlines below to practically implement on keys from this section. As you decorate the shapes, use an unusual tool, give yourself a limitation, intentionally make a mess, or come up with your own way to activate these ideas.

KEY COLLECTION ZONE

What ideas resonated with you most from this section? Use this space to record after your first reading and leave space to return and add keys you find as you continue your journey. These could be words to remember, ideas to revisit, or practical steps to take that apply these concepts.

CREATIVITY KEY

CREATIVITY KEY

CREATIVITY KEY

CREATIVITY GUIDE CORNER – Permission to Be in Process

Personal reflections to consider. Follow @one.step.growth on social media for more.

Pressure, stress, or less-than-ideal approaches can bog down the joy and momentum from creativity, even if you know your passions. This is a section to revisit often. I consistently find myself needing to make goals and plans more achievable or process the emotional side of creative expression. There are more small wins to celebrate than I often take time to see. Finding permission to continue to learn and grow in how I approach creativity has been crucial. As someone who used to be quite perfectionistic, the idea of looking at weaknesses in my own process used to be scary. My sobriety journey brought a shift, as I began to benefit from inputs and ideas shared that improved my approach to life.

Frame the keys from this section as self-awareness tips, momentum upgrades, creativity hacks, whatever helps you engage with them. As you'll read in future sections, the creative process is about connection, not perfection. It's okay if things get messy. I used to get sad about my weaknesses; now I can chuckle more about them. Not because there aren't costly moments or failure points, but because a lighter approach helps me maintain a growth mindset. As you take baby steps forward in exploring your expressions, you can experiment with your process too. Try implementing different keys in this section across various activities. Take note when things feel sensitive or hard; there may be something to explore. Staying connected to your inherent worth and value can increase openness to growth.

Chapter 5
HEALING

Stuck or slowed down and not sure why? Unprocessed pain can be a hindrance to creative progress, especially in meaningful expressions. Your natural state is to create. Apply tools that help you heal and move forward.

KEY CONCEPTS
Creativity Unlocked - Chapter 5

Hitting "Rocks" In Our Creative Journey

Rocks are a helpful metaphor for understanding how pain affects creativity. Whether the size of a mountain or a pebble lodged in a shoe, they can significantly hinder one's journey. Both rocks and pain can be formed by fiery moments, battering opposition by external forces, layers of accumulated muck compressed together, or intense pressure. They can turn an otherwise fun adventure into a disaster via a surprising slip or collision. Though the characteristics of a rock do impact the wound and specific solutions required, they don't change the fact that something needs to be addressed. A small stone can be just as deadly as a rockslide if experienced in a particular manner. Unresolved pain of any size can affect your creativity. It may be an unrealized force limiting your journey.

If finding delight or meaning in your expressions is difficult, take inventory of possible sources of pain related to a particular activity or creativity more broadly. Past experiences of difficulty and disappointment can cause hesitancy, pressure, and other challenges that impact your present emotions and process. You don't have to be a superhero. You have permission to raise your hand and say, "This hurts, and I need support." It's a brave, honest step that can transform your experiences. You may be facing a big rock that requires support beyond the tools offered in this book. That's okay. Other excavators, surgeons, and healers may be needed, like support groups or counselors and therapists. Take heart: healing is possible. In learning how to navigate the rocks in your creative journey, you just might discover tools and experiences that invigorate your life. At any point, feel free to step away and take a deep breath. Come up for air and connect to healthy forms of comfort and fun as needed.

Past pain may have led you to subconsciously limit aspects of your creative identity and expression. Even that which seems innocuous to another person can play a significant role. The effects of discouragement from a loved one, perceived failure during a performance, or a general sense of inadequacy can stick with us. Why do varying forms of pain affect us so differently? The sting can stay with us because of how we processed, or did not process, the triggered emotions. A 2007 UCLA study using brain scans showed that simply vocalizing negative emotions experienced can decrease the pain one feels, creating a therapeutic effect.* Acknowledging and speaking out what has been hard helps it not get stuck within. Places of unprocessed pain may not be directly related to a particular creative expression. The rocks may have formed via moments that don't seem connected but that left behind residual beliefs rooted in unworthiness, hopelessness, or self-hatred. Your sense of identity and worth impacts your words, voice, actions, desires, and other forms of self-expression.

*Source: Matthew D. Lieberman, Naomi I. Eisenberger, Molly J. Crockett, Sabrina M. Tom, Jennifer H. Pfeifer, and Baldwin M. Way (2007), "Putting Feels Into Words: Affect Labeling Disrupts Amygdala Activity in Response to Affective Stimuli," *Psychological Science*, accessed May 20, 2022. http://pss.sagepub.com/content/18/5/421.

This is not just an intellectual, factual understanding of yourself, but one that is deeply rooted and experienced in your emotions and your beliefs. There is good news: pain communicates a need for change. It is a signal, a call, an invitation for something new, for help, for comfort, for healing. Nobody can change the past; however, you can change how you see the past and how it affects you today.

Keys for Healing that Empower Creativity

I'm sorry that you have felt what you have felt, that your creativity was diminished, undervalued, squelched, or worse. That is not how you should have been treated. May your heart receive the warmth and love it needs in the midst of the pain it has known. You may need someone in person to speak similar words to you, whether once or again and again. Our hearts need comfort. They need a safe space for authentic expression of what they have experienced. Verifying the specific factual details of moments is not the priority in this personal process. Allowing the subjective, emotional experiences to be expressed is key for healing. And it leads into the tool that will help us move forward in the process: forgiveness.

The practice of forgiveness helps us accept our own imperfect humanity and that of others. It does not lessen the wrong committed or ignore the pain experienced. It is a letting go that actually frees us from the burdens of resentment, judgment, and guilt. The person who rejected, criticized, hurt, or disappointed you, knowingly or unknowingly, can be forgiven with or without direct communication. You can also forgive and still put in place practical changes and boundaries that are best for everyone's well-being, including your own. Forgiveness is the antidote for the poison of bitterness, which robs our present and future if unaddressed. Love is a more powerful motivator for our creativity than anger or fear, because sooner or later the latter will drain us. A meta-analysis of studies found that decreases in creative capacity are linked to experiences of stress specifically tied to a sense of uncontrollability over a situation or judgment from others.** There are parts of life where the best thing to do is to let go.

Forgiveness is a tool for addressing these experiences that we cannot change or that have contributed to a sense of shame or diminished identity or value. "Whether I forgive or don't forgive isn't going to affect whether justice is done," according to psychology professor Everett Worthington. "Forgiveness happens inside my skin."*** One key for activating greater capacity in this area is to recognize where we have received this gift ourselves. Consider where people chose to love and walk with you when you were behaving poorly. Think about moments where others saw the beauty in you and did not define you by your worst decisions. This is often a form of grace: undeserved love and connection in the midst of imperfection. Its generous nature can inspire change, and it can empower forgiveness of self and others.

**Source: Oshin Vartanian, Sidney Ann Saint, Nicole Herz, and Peter Suedfeld (2020), "The Creative Brain under Stress: Considerations for Performance in Extreme Environments." Frontiers in Psychology 11: 585969, accessed March 2022. https://doi.org/10.3389/ fpsyg.2020.585969

***Source: L. Toussaint, et al. (2016), "Effects of lifetime stress exposure on mental and physical health in young adulthood: How stress degrades and forgiveness protects health," Journal of Health Psychology, 21(6), 1004–1014, accessed Feburary 2022. https://doi. org/10.1177/1359105314544132 https://pubmed.ncbi.nlm.nih. gov/25139892/

JOURNAL PROMPT
Creativity Unlocked – Chapter 5

MEMORIES TO PAPER

Grab a journal and find a place where you feel comfortable and won't be interrupted. Reflect on the following questions. You may not have answers for all of them. Feel free to follow the flow as long as it's not overwhelming and to lean into thoughts, memories, or emotions that come up. Allow yourself to steer away from the questions and focus on what's happening inside of you as needed.

- What's a creative area that you feel blocked or delayed in?

- What's one creative expression that you loved but no longer use? When did you stop practicing it?

- Where have you experienced negative feelings, judgment, or self-criticism toward your expressions?

- Are there memories, events, or words tied to these perspectives?

- How have past experiences impacted what you believe about yourself and your creativity?

Grab an additional piece of paper if you run out of space. Write out your reflections in as much detail as you need. You don't have to analyze or fully understand them. Express the feelings you had during the moment, or that you are feeling while reflecting on the events.

JOURNAL PROMPT
Creativity Unlocked – Chapter 5

MEMORIES TO PAPER

After you've answered those questions, finish your journaling exercise by completing these last, important reflections.

If you could decide, what would you want to believe about yourself and your creative expressions instead?

_____

_____

_____

Is there a new perspective you need to embrace, a burden to let go, or someone you need to forgive? It could be yourself.

_____

_____

_____

If so, write out in your own words an expression of these thoughts.

_____

_____

_____

_____

_____

_____

ACTIVATION EXERCISE
Creativity Unlocked – Chapter 5

REACHING OUT

You don't have to do it alone. *The Grief Recovery Handbook* by John W. James and Russell Friedman explains that it's nearly impossible to effectively deal with grief of any kind by yourself.* Grief does not only happen when you lose a loved one or suffer a clear, significant tragedy. It's also the emotional impact of abruptly having to relocate or change jobs, or realizing you lost a piece of yourself when you were hurt in your creativity. All forms of grief need the listening ear and comfort of another human being. If you have an emotionally supportive friend or family member, reach out to them this week to share your findings of the journaling exercise. Ask them to listen to your memory and the impact it has had on you without giving advice or brushing it aside. If you're not sure how they'll respond, let them know beforehand that the most healing and helpful thing they can do is simply take the time to listen and validate your experience, even if they don't fully understand it.

If you feel overwhelmed by emotions or if you were triggered by a memory, don't hesitate to reach out for professional help. When past pain surfaces, many people need someone experienced to help them navigate through it. Your healing and breakthrough are closer than you think, and you're not on your own.

Action Plan

The situation or area where I'm seeking healing is: _____

My next step for addressing creative pain is: _____

The person that I will reach out to is: _____

One way I'm going to treat myself today is: _____

Check this box when you have completed each step above.

*James John W and Frank Cherry. The Grief Recovery Handbook : A Step-By-Step Program for Moving Beyond Loss. 1st Perennial Library ed. Harper & Row 19891988.

KEY COLLECTION ZONE

What ideas resonated with you most from this section? Use this space to record after your first reading and leave space to return and add keys you find as you continue your journey. These could be words to remember, ideas to revisit, or practical steps to take that apply these concepts.

CREATIVITY KEY

CREATIVITY KEY

CREATIVITY KEY

 ### CREATIVITY GUIDE CORNER – Regular "Rock" Removal
Personal reflections to consider. Follow @one.step.growth on social media for more.

Life has a way of bringing up "rocks," or pains, that have hindered our creative journeys in unexpected ways. On a recent flight I had a surprising realization. In a conversation with a high school student about his passion for law and translating that into a career, we talked about how one can feel limited in particular expressions via comparison if they have a family member already active in that field. As we descended toward Seattle's twinkling lights, I realized that I had held myself back from expressions in a certain industry because I didn't think I could live up to the success others achieved. A belief that I would need to surpass their experience and other associations with pain were limiting my freedom and confidence to create. Realizing this provided an invitation to implement the tools of this module again: processing pain, receiving comfort, forgiveness, and creating afresh.

This module is less about uprooting all aspects of pain that impact creativity right now and more about developing a process to address "rocks" when they arise. As I completed the writing of *Creativity Unlocked*, I realized that my struggle with loving my own voice started much earlier than the high school rejection I had previously pinpointed. From age 2 to 6, I didn't have my two front teeth. The resulting mispronunciations and shame from those experiences contributed to me becoming a very shy child and not believing in my voice. Recognizing this additional source of pain helped initiate deeper creative healing.

Chapter 6
COMMUNITY

Creativity thrives in community that celebrates and brings together individual gifts. But people can also cause pain that keeps us blocked. Discover a practical framework for navigating community and creativity well.

KEY CONCEPTS
Creativity Unlocked – Chapter 6

The Myth of Isolated Creators

If you wanted to make the objectively best, most flavorful beef taco (if such a designation could exist), you're likely going to need help. You may have the best carne asada preparation in the world, but you would be missing out if you didn't include your colleague's killer tortillas or your friend's amazing salsa. Here's the point: we are designed to create with others and benefit from the ingredients or tools they carry. The most impactful, lovely, sustainable outflows of creativity are often developed through community.

Intrinsic motivation for your creativity doesn't have to translate to isolation. The overly self-reliant, "I've got this on my own" attitude around your expressions will not serve you in the long run. Healthy community covers our weaknesses, celebrates our strengths, increases our resilience, and makes the journey so much more fun. In movies and culture, creative genius is often depicted in solitary, elusive individuals who eke out an isolated, pained existence. You know the type: the poet living in an attic, heroically baring their tortured soul on the page or the brilliant scientist who loves his chemicals and petri dishes more than people. These images are emphasized to the point that many associate loneliness, depression, pain, and coping mechanisms with "successful" creativity. But these patterns don't have to define your process.

I have great news: you do not have all of the ideas, answers, resources, or inspiration needed for many flourishing outflows of your creativity. You are designed to create with others, whether directly or indirectly. Your creativity isn't inferior if it involves partnership or draws inspiration from the artists or makers you appreciate. The outflow of any person is influenced and shaped by what they admire and experience. To think that we can somehow create without any attachment to previous works or other people is a bit ludicrous. Who made the paints or tools you're using? Who developed the concepts, spaces, or genres that inspire your expressions? We get to be part of the perpetually growing sculpture of human creativity. At some point, others will be able to stand on our shoulders. Take a deep breath. Let go of the measuring stick; allow the pressure of originality and self-reliance to roll off your shoulders. Trade it for the joy of creative community. It's not meant to all be on you—it never was.

Numerous research studies have highlighted that healthy, long-lasting relationships with other people are what are associated with flourishing and happiness in life. Creativity offers opportunities for building life-giving, long-term communities that support your holistic wellbeing. Regular interactions in groups with shared passions can spark relationship with others, especially where there is alignment in values. Whether you connect via skydiving or student teaching, electric vehicles or emo rock, entrepreneurship or a social cause, important intangible needs can be met through the friendships developed.

Upgrading Your Creative Community

A creative community is not required to start exploring and enjoying your expressions. Seasons of independence can be important for experimentation, practice, and growth. Some parts of your journey may feel too vulnerable to share initially, especially in contexts that are complex or with expressions that are deeply personal. But, at the right time, community is valuable for helping you see problems differently, identify solutions, and navigate the emotions of the process. If you're feeling stuck or frustrated, the keys you need may lie in others.

At the most basic level, a creative community consists of the people whom you choose to involve in your journey. It often extends beyond a single group of people and will be different for various expressions. Your community might be a mixture of friends, family, colleagues, mentors, clubs, collaborators, and others who support your journey. Some you may choose to invite while others may have a more indirect role or already be part of your process. Not every person or group you include will be the right fit for you or be part of your journey forever. If a partnership doesn't work out, don't fret! A different individual or approach may be needed.

As you read these words, you might already be sensing an important tension. Community holds great benefit for the creative process, yet many of the painful experiences discussed in the previous section were caused by other people. It's possible to access the benefits of collaboration and encouragement while reducing unnecessary cycles of difficulty. Some of the fear or hesitancy that people experience around creating with others isn't actually of community. It's actually a fear of repeating pain or disappointment they have experienced in past moments. The tools in this section are designed to help navigate this tension with clarity.

Your creative community will be most life-giving when your needs are aligned with the roles and capacity of individuals, and vice versa. For instance, a newfound passion for visual art would benefit from a different form of community than a desire to explore activities that strengthen relationships with one's teenage children. Finding an appropriate level of skill and time commitment is also important. When you're starting out, resist the pressure to jump into something that could leave you overwhelmed and discouraged. There is no shame in signing up for a beginners group. You can also take a baby-steps approach in the emotional aspects of building trust with your creative community. Just because someone shares your interest in Picasso doesn't mean they're the right person to tell your deepest fears or dreams.

Thinking about four specific roles for others in your creative process will help you structure community. *(1) Community for consistency.* Early in exploring a creative expression, find people who encourage you to regularly invest time and persevere in your efforts, like a workshop or peer group, without needing to share output. *(2) Community for processing.* As you progress, the creative journey will cause fears, insecurities, and negative belief systems to come up. A friend, mentor, class, or group can help you healthily process your thoughts and emotions. *(3) Community for collaboration.* Partner with others who can expand the depth, range, and excellence of your outflows and help you weather difficult moments. Look for those who add momentum, ideas, or fun. *(4) Community for feedback.* When you're ready, pursue specific input and ideas from others that can help you refine your craft or see things in a different light.

JOURNAL PROMPT
Creativity Unlocked – Chapter 6

MAPPING OUT CURRENT CREATIVE COMMUNITY

The people, tools, and groups needed to strengthen community around your expressions depends on your stage and unique story. The first step to growth is recognizing who and what is involved currently in your creative outflows. Read through the examples below and then use the table on the next page to map out your current community for three expressions you want to prioritize. There may be boxes you leave blank. Think outside-the-box: you can include YouTube channels, apps, or other resources that support your journey.

Example 1: Writing Children's Books - Goals: Fun, Self-Expression, Possible Future Income

- *Consistency:* Weekly writing times scheduled on calendar; Cori, a neighbor who I told about the project
- *Processing:* My significant other; the members of a regional writers' club group I visit monthly
- *Collaboration:* Sam, a friend who has volunteered to sketch visual ideas for the story; my writing MasterClass or Creativity Unlocked Workshop instructor
- *Feedback:* Test readers, editors (in the future)

Example 2: Going on Camping Adventures - Goals: Community, Joy, Exercise

- *Consistency:* A group of friends who have decided to complete a camping trip every quarter
- *Processing:* A buddy, family member, or coach who will listen to the highs and lows of my camping adventures
- *Collaboration:* Rob, who is eager to share planning duties and explore new locations and campfire cooking solutions
- *Feedback:* YouTube channels teaching new campfire cooking techniques; trip attendees

Example 3: Pursuing a New Career in Tech or Sales - Goals: Better Income, Less Boredom

- *Consistency:* Roommates or community group members who encourage me in the process
- *Processing:* A mentor or coach helping guide me through the journey
- *Collaboration:* One former colleague introducing me to possible employers or training programs; a friend helping review a resume
- *Feedback:* A former manager or boss willing to give input; educational courses or bootcamps helping build skillset

JOURNAL PROMPT
Creativity Unlocked – Chapter 6

MAPPING OUT CURRENT CREATIVE COMMUNITY

Expression	example: writing and singing music		
Consistency	example: lessons with Michaela		
Processing	example: Laura, mentor, and friends		
Collaboration	example: Ted, Kevin, and Sarah; partner from a music class		
Feedback	example: a local producer; a MasterClass group		
Past or Current Goals for Expression	example: self-expression, joy		

ACTIVATION EXERCISE
Creativity Unlocked – Chapter 6

ONE SQUARE AT THE TIME: UPGRADING COMMUNITY

Now, it's time to further build or upgrade your creative community. Use the table on the next page to brainstorm ideas for individuals, groups, or tools that could support growth. Include the people and resources already involved that you want to keep but focus on identifying new possibilities. Leave off those that you decide no longer are a good fit. Fill in as many squares you would like to initially, and feel free to return and add more any time.

Once you have completed the table, brainstorm and start completing three follow-up actions: one for today, one for this week, and one for later this month. Pick up the phone to call a person you have in mind, sign up for a workshop, become a member of a club, search for a coach online, join a Facebook group and introduce yourself, clarify your vision with a current collaborator, or something else. The right next step may be not be a formal request for partnership or an intensive conversation. It might be simply spending time with someone to strengthen a relationship or finding a way to involve yourself in what they're doing. One of the best ways to learn from those further along than us is to serve something they're creating. If you're having trouble getting started, choose a square that feels like a more fun or easy step. Some doors may not open now. That's okay. Keep looking for a step you can take. Revisit this tool over the coming months to brainstorm more ideas for upgrading your community.

Action Step Example 1: Writing Children's Books

- *Consistency:* Set up a daily calendar reminder and a weekly check-in call with a friend.
- *Processing:* Schedule a regular coaching session to address imposter syndrome.
- *Collaboration:* Join an online writing club to share work and ask for input.
- *Refinement:* Find an editor who can offer deep, constructive, honest feedback on a draft.

Action Step Example 2: Camping

- *Consistency:* Set aside the first weekend of every month to go camping with a friend. If schedules or weather conflict, schedule a make-up date or use that Saturday to plan.
- *Processing:* Tell a loved one or mentor about the highs and lows of your camping process.
- *Collaboration:* Have a regular hangout with friends who like the outdoors to share new locations and tips, and share stories and pictures from outdoor adventures.
- *Refinement:* Attend local or online workshops taught by outdoor experts, backpacking guides or park rangers to get trained on best practices and learn about new gear.

ACTIVATION EXERCISE
Creativity Unlocked – Chapter 6

ONE SQUARE AT THE TIME: UPGRADING COMMUNITY

Expression	ex: singing			
Consistency	ex: lessons with Michaela			
Processing	ex: Laura, mentor, and friends			
Collaboration	ex: Ted, Kevin, and Sarah			
Feedback	ex: producer			
Current or Future for Goals for Expression	ex: local coffee shop			

KEY COLLECTION ZONE

What ideas resonated with you most from this section? Use this space to record after your first reading and leave space to return and add keys you find as you continue your journey. These could be words to remember, ideas to revisit, or practical steps to take that apply these concepts.

CREATIVITY KEY

_____

_____

CREATIVITY KEY

_____

_____

CREATIVITY KEY

_____

_____

 **CREATIVITY GUIDE CORNER – Better Together... Really!**
Personal reflections to consider. Follow @one.step.growth on social media for more.

For years, I thought that I had to be somehow uniquely original or impactful for my creativity to matter. That pressure hindered my expressions and robbed me of joy. Walls went up that blocked opportunities to learn from or partner with others because I was afraid or felt like I had to "prove myself." If this resonates with you, it's not too late to make a change. You can trade the made-up requirements of creative originality and mastery for a prioritization of joy and connection. This shift can actually fuel greater excellence and authenticity by removing pressure and increasing delight that sparks action and practice. For me, this shift in goals increased freedom of expression and opened doors for collaboration in art, business, writing, and other arenas. Community now fuels my process.

For all the benefits of creating together, it can still hold challenges. I have invited people into projects that have not been an ideal fit and been through some hard conversations. You're not going to get it right all the time. People are messy (including me). Healthy boundaries, communication techniques, and conflict resolution skills can be strengthened through creating in community. There is uncertainty in most choices around collaboration because there are many unknown factors. I have found that taking small steps over time, having a plan if things don't work out, and looking for values alignment to be helpful in applying these concepts. When things get hard, take time to rest and get refreshed.

Chapter 7
CONNECTION

The relationships we have with ourselves, others, and something greater than ourselves can fuel our creativity with inspiration and energy. Or they can hinder it. Learn how to refresh your expressions with meaningful connection.

KEY CONCEPTS
Creativity Unlocked - Chapter 7

The Secret Sauce for Creative Expression

Think of a moment when you felt profound joy or satisfaction. You know, those times when your skin tingles, colors appear a little brighter, joy seeps through your emotions, and the world seems full of wonder. Where have you experienced these sensations? What were you doing? Who were you with? What do you remember most?

Chances are that you were creating, whether a memory, a piece of art, a deeper relationship with someone, a tangible product, or something else. Think of a few other moments where you experienced similar sensations. Can you spot any commonalities? They are part of your creative nature, but what else? The truth is that the meaning, joy, and happiness we discover through our creative nature is rooted in experiences of genuine connection. Contrary to the messages that dominate our culture, these occurrences are not dependent on social media-worthy settings or expensive purchases. Powerful, heart-alive moments of creativity can happen in almost any context when we experience life-giving connection with our own voice or passions, others, or something greater than us. This approach makes life a canvas full of possibility.

Connection is in the flash of an idea interrupting your routine and ushering in a flow of details and solutions for a previously unaddressed challenge. It's in the waves of beautiful emotion that swell and crest amongst a concert audience, linking together hearts full of wonder via sounds that move the human soul. It's in the sympathetic smile of a stranger in a subway station after you have trudged through a downpour and now look like a drowned rat. It's in crafting a work of art that sparks ecstatic joy and offers to an unsuspecting world a new, visual representation of grief and hope. It's in the satisfaction of an Excel formula or financial ledger finally balancing, or the selection of the right accent color for your living room. It's in the moments of learning you share with a family member, and the deep conversations that occur around late night campfires.

Defining and Activating Multiple Forms of Connection

Meaningful connection takes many forms, inhabits many channels, and fills our hearts in ways beyond our ability to describe with words. This intangible but oh-so-real quality can spark intense spikes of joy or subtler, profound satisfaction. To help us recognize and experience more of this powerful quality, let's define meaningful connection. For simplicity's sake, we will use three categories. A first form of connection is with other people. In her book *The Gifts of Imperfection*, noted author and researcher Dr. Brené Brown defines connection as "the energy that exists between people when they feel seen, heard, and valued; when they can give and receive without judgment; and when they derive sustenance and strength from the relationship."* It's the foundation of authentic, life-giving relationship.

*Source: Brené Brown, *The Gifts of Imperfection* (Hazelden Information & Educational Services, 2010).

A second bucket is connection with self. It involves elements of self-realization, awareness of one's needs, and individuality. We can apply part of Dr. Brown's definition from above: healthy connection with ourselves is the energy that exists when we can see, hear, and value ourselves, when we can express ourselves and rest without judgment, and when our relationships with ourselves add strength and positive qualities to our lives. This includes recognizing our unique personality, gifts, and perspectives, as well as taking care of our selves physically, emotionally, and mentally. Meaningful, authentic expression flows best from a foundation of wellness.

A third form of connection is with something greater than us. This could be in the form of values, a higher power, nature, spirituality or faith, or a cause that provides a sense of purpose and place in the world. Examples of practical experiences include the satisfaction of contributing to a movement or charitable organization, meaningful religious experiences, getting lost in the beauty of the outdoors, or expressing kindness to someone needing help. As life progresses, there can be a need deeper experiences and additional sources of connection.

Connection Fuels a Flourishing Life

Why should we care about connection? There is a growing collection of research that suggests its various forms hold great importance for health and happiness. Examples include a Harvard study on happiness that showed the association of long-term relationships with satisfaction, Dr. Brené Brown's work on improved life outcomes and vulnerability, research on mindfulness practices, the emotional health benefits of spending time in nature, or the positive associations of participation in a religious group with well-being and other metrics.

In addition to supporting wellness, meaningful connection supercharges creativity. Your heart-alive experiences of expressions have likely involved aspects of this quality, whether or not it was recognized. For instance, those moments could have included an activity rooted in your passions and unique skills, an adventure that sparked friendship, an authentic artistic expression, a glorious nature scene, a life-giving spiritual practice, a solution to a complicated problem that affects your customers, or an important cause or community. If your creative process has become stale, you might need to find a fresh experience of meaningful connection on one of the levels described above. Taking care of your self, activating a new gift, a conversation with a mentor, or mindfulness can spark fresh inspiration and momentum.

Experiences where connection is lacking further prove its importance. Have you carefully planned something you hoped to be wonderful only for the actual experience to feel hollow and unfulfilling? Chances are there was some form of disconnection present. The absence of connection can reduce the delight and fulfillment that creative adventures provide. For instance, the meal at a great restaurant or the dream vacation may promise enjoyment but leave you dissatisfied when you're fighting with your significant other. A work promotion or the latest footwear may have limited joy when it's not rooted in connection with your priorities. Moments of fun or achievement aren't bad, but they can be fleeting and leave us endlessly needing more if we aren't experiencing healthy connection on the levels described above.

JOURNAL PROMPT
Creativity Unlocked – Chapter 7

REFLECT ON CONNECTION

You can choose one or both or the journaling prompts below. The first is more practical, while the second is an opportunity to be more reflective, philosophical, or spiritual. Take fifteen minutes to reflect and write about the following.

Option One:
Make a list of three creative experiences that were disappointing or produced negative sentiments, and three that were positive and life-giving. Try to find common elements within both sets of moments. How was connection present or lacking? How did that affect your experience? Were there moments when pressure or expectations towards yourself or others got in the way of being present, connected, and even vulnerable?

Option Two:
Write out a paragraph or two answering the following questions: how do you see creativity as a channel for deeper connection in your life? How has or can connection inspire your creativity? Consider all the elements of connection: with yourself and your story, with the people around you, and with something greater than yourself. You may not know the answer when you start writing. Put the pen to paper, and see what flows out.

ACTIVATION EXERCISE
Creativity Unlocked – Chapter 7

UPGRADING CONNECTION

Close your eyes and take a deep breath. Ask yourself the question: "with whom or what do I need to connect with the most this week?" Don't think about who you "should" connect with, or what is required by your responsibilities or calendar. Allow your heart to identify what it needs the most right now. This could be a specific person or a group of people, but it could also be the connection with yourself, a higher power, or something gives a sense of purpose or place in the world. Don't overthink it; go with the first thing that came to mind. Now clear out an evening or a morning this week to pursue this connection through a creative expression.

Here are a few examples:
- Plan a night with a friend or loved one where you turn your phones off to cook a new dish.
- Go for a hike by yourself or with a group of friends, depending on your needs.
- Carve out time to rest, watch a favorite movie, exercise, or practice another form of self-care.
- Play a silly game with your children.
- Teach a neighbor some of your handyman skills as you build something together.
- Share one of your poems at an open mic night or support group meeting.
- Feel permission to work on your side hustle or passion project that isn't about the money.
- Allow your heart to express itself while plucking away at the strings of your guitar.
- Listen to a meditation, spiritual reading, or song while you paint.

Once you pick your activation, write it out in the lines below. Then, add it to one of the blank lines in the Disconnection Troubleshooter tool on the following page. The main purpose of this exercise is not to improve an expression, but to practice sparking deeper connection via creativity that can refresh your journey. Look for ways within and outside of your routine.

ACTIVATION EXERCISE
Creativity Unlocked – Chapter 7
THE DISCONNECTION TROUBLESHOOTER

Use this tool to consider the current state of connection in your life on multiple levels. Write a number in each box (1 = weak, 10 = strong) and circle or write in action steps. The goal is authenticity, not to have a high score. Within each category, there will be some areas that are more of a challenge, hard to change, or lower than others. That's okay. Revisit this tool when you feel creatively stuck or tired to identify ways to spark fresh connection and fuel your journey.

YOURSELF

Rate your connection to yourself (1-10):

Sleep/Rest ☐   Food & Hydration ☐

Exercise ☐   Passion & Purpose ☐

Mental & Emotional Health ☐   Spiritual Wellness ☐

Choose two activations to prioritize:

- Take a nap
- Go on a walk
- Plan a trip
- Watch a movie
- Set an alarm
- _____
- _____

- Read a book
- Take a nap
- Meet a counselor
- Personality test
- Listen to music
- _____
- _____

OTHERS

Rate your connection with others (1-10):

Fun Friendships ☐   Emotional Processing Friends ☐

Family ☐   Work or School Connections ☐

Hobby Groups ☐   Other Community Activities ☐

Choose 2 activations to prioritize:

- Schedule a coffee
- Send thankful text
- Write a note
- Call a friend
- Join club or group
- _____
- _____

- Gratitude affirmations
- Meal w / coworker
- Go to an event
- Plan a trip
- See a counselor
- _____
- _____

GREATER THAN US

Rate connection to something greater (1-10):

Issue, Topic, or Cause ☐   Alignment with Personal Values ☐

Community ☐   Sense of Purpose ☐

Faith & Spirituality ☐   Mission-Focused Organization ☐

Choose 2 activations to prioritize::

- Reflect
- Nature time
- Pray / meditate
- Volunteer
- Ask forgiveness
- _____
- _____

- Talk with friend
- Attend service
- Give time or $$
- Journal
- Make amends
- _____
- _____

KEY COLLECTION ZONE

What ideas resonated with you most from this section? Use this space to record after your first reading and leave space to return and add keys you find as you continue your journey. These could be words to remember, ideas to revisit, or practical steps to take that apply these concepts.

CREATIVITY KEY

CREATIVITY KEY

CREATIVITY KEY

 **CREATIVITY GUIDE CORNER – What It's All About**
Personal reflections to consider. Follow @one.step.growth on social media for more.

This. This. This. The essence of life is meaningful connection. One of the biggest discoveries in my life was that this positive energy that fuels life-giving creativity can be found every day, in unexpected settings from grocery stores to recovery meetings. For me, deeper levels of spiritual connection and vulnerable, authentic relationship brought a sense of being fully alive. The contentment and joy surpassed what I had found in impact and service, educational achievement, traveling the world, or career advancement. None of these are bad. But at times I found them depressingly hollow due to unmet needs for connection. Life stripped down to the basics can reveal what matters more and what matters less. Even if you don't agree with or believe this concept right away, give it a try. When connection is the focus, seemingly long journeys in your expressions become more fueled and fun.

When I returned to the corporate world with this new focus on connection, I was surprised to discover how different and life-giving my experience could be. I tapped into moments of relational connection in the office, personal and spiritual connection on my commutes, and new hobbies connected to authentic interests and creative passions. A cause bigger than myself helped clarify next steps in my career. The truth is that for many of us this approach can seem foreign. Modern culture teaches us to focus on output or achievement over the connection that the process can hold. But you can take a different, more fulfilling path.

Chapter 8
BELIEFS

Your philosophical or spiritual beliefs about yourself and the world impact your experience of creativity. Discover how exploration and incremental shifts can better support your creative dreams and goals.

KEY CONCEPTS
Creativity Unlocked – Chapter 8

The Inevitable Impact of Beliefs

Perspectives about the big questions and intangible aspects of life influence one's creativity. Philosophies and worldviews can strengthen helpful virtues like love and gratitude, or fuel experiences that keep one discouraged and stuck. It's harder to invest time and effort for long-term projects if your worldview doesn't provide hope for the present or future. Philosophical or religious belief can play an important role in the healing from past pain and experiences of meaningful connection that fuel creative exploration. Conversely, a sense of detachment on an existential level can rob our energy and hinder our expressions. Similar to mindsets, the specific beliefs we embrace have great importance. Studies have indicated an association between psychological safety and increased creative thought, while stressors that feel uncontrollable or tied to loss of social standing decrease it. Within both religious and nonreligious schools of thought, there are ideas that better support creativity than others.

We can have negative associations with the topic of beliefs due to previous difficult experiences. There may be philosophical, spiritual, or faith practices that once soured your taste or caused you pain, whether due to their substance or their association with a person or situation that hurt you. You may have an aversion to a belief system or philosophy due to the pain you felt for which no one ever apologized. Or you may have inherited a particular lean from a family member's previous experience. Barriers can also stem from difficult interactions with parents, teachers, or leaders, or your perception of events where it seemed like larger forces in the world, like systems and structures, or even God, failed you or others. Or there may have been an unrelated, co-occurring negative factor that shaped your perception of spirituality, like how catching a stomach virus can sour one's taste for a dish recently eaten.

There are benefits for your creativity in exploring new recipes, or a different chef, that help you broaden your palate again. Within worldviews that previously felt painful or spurred misunderstanding, there could be comfort for difficult experiences, inspiration for your expressions, and deeper connection and purpose. In the exploration process, it is worthwhile to consider both the tenets of a worldview or spiritual practice and other factors that may have hindered your previous experiences.

Not everything we associate with certain ideologies or faith traditions is actually core to its message. There are many with whom one may share a religion or philosophy but have profound disagreements on various topics, whether politics or interpretation of specific doctrines. But one's worldview can also make space for that process. We can see people with whom we disagree and still love one another and work to see the outflows of our shared humanity resemble the virtues we celebrate. Places of belief that used to hold pain, disappointment, and unanswered questions can also become opportunities for discovery.

JOURNAL PROMPT - PART 1
Creativity Unlocked - Chapter 8

A BELIEFS CHECK-IN

Sooner or later, you will arrive at a point where your creativity touches questions around beliefs and core values. This might spark from a moment of profound wonder or from a situation where ethical considerations are important in what you produce or how you make it. Human creative expression can release love or fear, light or darkness, beauty or destruction. How you see the world and what you believe about it will impact what you bring into existence.

Let's take some time to consider beliefs and how they are currently impacting your creative process. In the lines below or on a separate piece of paper, write out thoughts on the following:

- *What would you describe as your current worldview or values in a spiritual, religious, or philosophical sense?* This could be a specific tradition, a loosely formed set of ideas, or a conscious choice to believe in very little or the pointlessness of these questions.
- *How do ideals and practices of your beliefs inspire your expressions or inform your voice?* Where do you see your values fueling, hindering, or speaking through your creativity?
- *How does your belief system help you navigate ethical or relational tensions in your creative expressions?* Reflect on how your worldview and values guides your choices in challenges.
- *Are the core values of your beliefs helping you thrive?* Reflect on areas of wellness and relationships that could use strengthening. Is there a belief that could shift?

JOURNAL PROMPT - PART 2
Creativity Unlocked - Chapter 8

THE CONSISTENCY OF CHANGE

Picture yourself at a younger age, sometime in your teenage years or earlier. Think about what you used to believe then. Reflect for a minute or two on a few ways that has changed.
Life experiences profoundly impact our hearts and our belief systems, for better or worse. For some of us, our connection to certain ideologies or approaches is more emotional and less logical than we realize. These shifts can support or restrict the joy, connection, and momentum we find in our expressions. Use the lines below or a separate piece of paper to reflect on questions that will help you explore how your worldview and creativity can continue to evolve.

- *Where have beliefs about your creativity shifted in recent seasons?* Are there expressions or aspects of your own gifts or potential that you now see differently?
- *What are one or two things that you used to believe about life that you don't currently?* Where have experiences shifted your worldview? What questions spark tension or mystery?
- *Where has a philosophy, belief system, or spiritual or religious practice been soured by past or present pain?* Have there been difficulties that built barriers to certain schools of thought?
- *What aspects of your philosophy or spirituality could be further explored or deepened?* Are there places where your experience of a worldview isn't producing the fruits that you seek?
- *What are the values and beliefs of the people who inspire you?* Is there something you could glean from those who carry the attributes you admire?

ACTIVATION EXERCISE
Creativity Unlocked – Chapter 8

CONNECT CREATIVITY AND BELIEF

Now, pretend like you could travel a decade into the future and that you're answering questions as yourself but 10 years older. How do you experience your worldview, faith, beliefs, or spirituality now? What has changed? What have you discovered? How is your creativity and your connection with yourself and others fueled by your connection to a higher purpose, a philosophy, or a faith or spiritual practice? Include something that is different and more positive than what you believe today, whether about yourself, your creativity, or the world around you. Describe it as if you're telling a future friend, using present tense and specific descriptions.

When you feel discouraged or disconnected from a sense of purpose, this description of a future life of belief and creativity can serve as a reminder that things can change. Allow this vision of a possible future inspire you to keep exploring and refining. Remember: your beliefs, philosophy, or faith and spiritual practices will continue to be shaped by your experiences. Find what brings you a sense of hope and encouragement, and stay open to new discoveries. For more examples of how belief systems have impacted impactful creators or details around my own personal story of awakening and creativity, check out the chapter on spirituality in *Creativity Unlocked*.

ACTIVATION EXERCISE
Creativity Unlocked – Chapter 8

CONNECT CREATIVITY AND BELIEF

Pick a creative expression that you feel most comfortable with, or the one that you're currently most excited about. Come up with one way you can connect your spiritual or philosophical beliefs with this expression. Here are some examples:

- Listen to a guided creativity meditation before activating your expression
- Write a song, short play, or poem representing aspects of your worldview
- Experience a philosophical idea or piece that inspires you or share about one with a friend via conversation
- Hold a dance party for yourself with music that helps you feel spiritually connected
- Ask questions, whether through prayer, reflective journaling, or another practice, and look for answers that arise
- Collaborate with other spiritually-, philosophically-, or faith-minded people around your expression
- Find stories of creative heroes of yours and research their philosophy, worldview, or faith or spiritual practices, and how that affected their lives.
- Go on a solo outdoor adventure and enjoy the nature around you

Use the space below to write out what you choose. Once completed, add notes on the experiences, ideas, or questions that arise in the process.

KEY COLLECTION ZONE

What ideas resonated with you most from this section? Use this space to record after your first reading and leave space to return and add keys you find as you continue your journey. These could be words to remember, ideas to revisit, or practical steps to take that apply these concepts.

CREATIVITY KEY

_____

_____

CREATIVITY KEY

_____

_____

CREATIVITY KEY

_____

_____

CREATIVITY GUIDE CORNER – Believe It or Not
Personal reflections to consider. Follow @one.step.growth on social media for more.

Santa Claus. The tooth fairy. Certain investment strategies. Who is trustworthy. What matters most in our lives. Our understanding of ourselves and the world around us is constantly shifting. Think back to some of the things that you used to believe that now make you chuckle. Instead of getting down about those thoughts, celebrate that what you believe about yourself, your creativity, and the world can change--for the better! Seven years ago, I would have been shocked by what I believe presently about myself and my creativity. Small steps to explore new experiences -- many that seemed too good to be true -- have contributed to full grown beliefs that empower creative adventures. I am a songwriter. I am worthy of love. My voice is not less-than; it carries a beautiful uniqueness. My messy past doesn't get to define my future. I am a leader, and I can lead with joy. Shifting from pressure and shame to a more wholehearted approach enabled me to embrace these beliefs, which are beyond what I would have thought possible.

Belief flows out of our inner being, what some people might one's heart, soul, or gut. You might be a person who deeply values spirituality or faith. Or you might be someone whose core belief is that logic and scientific facts are the best or only ways to process the world. Either way, it's helpful to recognize that we all have beliefs that shape us. Exploring these intangible aspects of the human experience can aid your creativity, and vice-versa.

Chapter 9
CHILDLIKENESS

Do you want to grow in confidence, ideation, or delight in your creativity? These are all aspects of childlikeness, which is a key for creative flow. Apply science-inspired tools to enhance this quality and your expression.

KEY CONCEPTS
Creativity Unlocked – Chapter 9

Celebrating the Child Within

Rediscovering the attributes of childlikeness is rocket fuel for creativity. Healthy kids possess imagination, permission for self-expression, and ease in accessing joy that would benefit many adults. Several decades ago, NASA partnered with researchers to measure the creativity of prospective astronauts. The developers of the resulting test decided to also measure this quality across different age groups. They found that young kids naturally exhibit incredibly high levels of creativity. However, it appears to sharply diminish as they get older—98 percent of five-year-old children scored highly on their measures, but that percentage decreased to only 30 percent of ten-year-olds, 12 percent of fifteen-year-olds, and 2 percent of adults.*

Children raised in supportive contexts possess qualities that allow for creative flow to spark. This section is not an invitation to the stubbornness, inflexibility, or demanding personality associated with childishness. Rather, it's a celebration of positive qualities enabled by healthy development. Safety and security allows curiosity, expression, and imagination. Here are more of the qualities that increasing childlikeness can add to your creative journey:

Joy and delight	*Fun, play, and spontaneity*
Flexibility and resourcefulness	*Permission for learning and mystery*
Confidence to dream	*Abundance thinking and generosity*
Experimentation and outside-the-box thinking	*Resilience and perseverance*

How do we proactively increase childlikeness for our expressions? Breaking out of "stuck" mindsets, like "this is just how it is," requires intention. We also may need help to address past pain that has robbed us of these qualities. Groundbreaking research in the late 1980s revealed for the first time the long-lasting impact of adverse childhood experiences throughout life. Despite these challenges, the brain's neuroplastic nature means that there is potential for change, no matter one's age. We are developing patterns continually, whether it's reinforcing existing ones or intentionally learning new ones that better serve our journey.

Application of practices from early childhood development can help unlock creativity. When kids are protected, nourished, cared for, educated, encouraged, and given healthy guidance, they develop confidence, security, skills, and the motivation to pursue their dreams. Research has shown that higher levels of serotonin, a calming neurotransmitter, are associated with increased creative thought.** Experiences of childlikeness make space to explore and grow.

*Source: Larry Vint (2005), "Fresh Thinking Drives Creativity Innovation," QUICK - Journal of the Queensland Society for Information Technology in Ed., No. 94, accessed 02/22. https://research-repository.griffith.edu.au/bitstream/handle/10072/7880/33187_1.pdf
**Source: Jandy Le, Michael Xiong, Joshi Jwalin (2019). "The Scientific Origin of Creativity," *Neurotech@Berkeley,* Dec. 10, 2019, accessed 06/23, https://medium.com/neurotech-berkeley/the-scientific-origin-of-creativity-587799f0fbe2.

JOURNAL PROMPT - PART 1
Creativity Unlocked - Chapter 9

CHILDLIKE CHARACTERISTICS

There are many childlike characteristics that enrich our creativity and lives:

- Unapologetic expression of preferences and dislikes
- Confidence
- Willingness to take risks
- Ability to create joy and play in the mundane

- A deep value for fun
- Flexibility
- Delight, wonder and openness
- Endless eagerness to learn, curiosity
- Ability to forgive quickly and trust again

What childlike characteristics do you already portray in your creativity or in life? List out at least two attributes you can celebrate. Which childlike characteristics do you want to develop more? How could upgrading them change your experiences of creativity?

_____

_____

_____

_____

_____

Reflecting on moments, settings or activities that help stir these qualities. Are there contexts where you find it easiest to be childlike? What helps each of us will vary.

_____

_____

_____

_____

JOURNAL PROMPT – PART 2
Creativity Unlocked – Chapter 9

UPGRADE YOUR CHILDLIKENESS

Keys from early childhood development best practices can help spark fresh experiences of creative flow. Experiences of safety, nourishment, and stage-appropriate challenges contribute to greater confidence, skills, and motivation around one's expressions. Brainstorm ideas around the five prompts below:

Upgrade external environment. How could you adjust your schedule to improve your creative process, or make your environment more aesthetically or emotionally supportive?

Make space for free expression. When can you make time to play, or to create without the weight of task lists, responsibilities, pressure, or even the need of a tangible outcome?

Experiment with new, stage-appropriate challenges. Where can you take on a task that is stretching but not overwhelming? How else can you position yourself to continue learning?

Stay creatively nourished. How will you get refreshed creatively this season? Is it via nature, viewing art, having fun experiences with friends, ensuring introvert time, or something else?

Strengthen internal environment. What affirmations or mindsets tools focused on joy, playfulness, confidence, wellness or other topics do you need to add to your routine?

ACTIVATION EXERCISE
Creativity Unlocked – Chapter 9

CHILDLIKE PLAY

It's time to play! Schedule some time for uninterrupted creative flow, preferably in a place where you can get messy. Pick one or more of the activities below and channel your inner five-year-old as you simply have fun without any other purpose or goal.

WILD OUT(FIT). Go to your local thrift store and find a wacky outfit that brings you joy. Break all the fashion rules, go for the flashiest colors and craziest patterns, or simply pick something unusual that makes you chuckle. Try it on and take pictures of yourself. If you're up for a real childlike challenge, buy the items and meet a friend for lunch or coffee while wearing these clothes.

CHUCKLE TUBE. Find a playlist of funny videos on YouTube and allow yourself to laugh as loud and as long as you need.

PAINTING BY HAND. Cover your table with one of those plastic tablecloths you can get at a dollar store. Grab some sheets of thick paper and a few tubes of cheap, water-soluble paint. Paint with fingers, or your whole hand, and dare to get messy! Remind yourself nobody will ever see the end result, so you don't have to make anything aesthetically pleasing. This is just about having fun!

MESSY ART. Cover an outdoor space with plastic or a tarp. Buy a large poster board or find a canvas in a thrift store. You could also repurpose old sheets or tablecloths in a pinch by pinning it to a wall or floor that's covered. Now, make your own masterpiece by throwing paint on it. Here's the rule: you cannot use brushes. Instead, play around with your hands, utensils, household items, or even water balloons or water guns (use diluted paint). The sky's the limit!

RE-PLAY. Get out a piece of sports equipment or game *that you haven't used in at* least three years and play for an hour. Find a friend or local group if needed.

FORT-ITUDE. Build a fort out of sheets and blankets and pillows in the living room and invite people over for a movie night. Or go next-level and build a make-shift fort from pallets and sheets in the backyard.

ACTIVATION EXERCISE
Creativity Unlocked - Chapter 9

UPPING THE ANTE WITH FRIENDS

If you have kids, a creative partner, or some friends who are well-advanced in childlikeness (pick that slightly "crazy" friend!), invite them to join. Here are some group activities that will guarantee laughter and silliness regardless of age!

EDI-BATTLE ROYALE. Find food items like flour, whipping cream, pudding, sauces, old vegetables spaghetti, eggs, and set them out on a table in your driveway or yard. Set a countdown, decide on some ground rules if necessary, and break out in an epic food fight! Pro tip: wear old clothes and have a garden hose nearby to rinse off.

WATER FIGHT. For a less messy version, get a few water guns and water balloons and have an epic water fight instead (or use snow if available). If you are close to a beach, creek or lake, let everyone cover themselves in mud before starting the water fight. The one that still has the most mud on their skin after the water fight wins!

CASTING CALL. Get a few party props or costumes out with friends or family, or purchase some outrageous clothing items at a local thrift store. Let everyone make their own crazy outfit. Go over-the-top with accessories or makeup. Once you've finalized your look, take your phone or camera and do a photoshoot together. Make the silliest face you can without pulling a muscle and strike a pose!

SPONTANEOUS ADVENTURE. Pile into a car with a few friends (with a legally-aged driver). Pick a number between 20 and 50 and then take turns picking the next turn or direction that the car should take: left, right, or continuing straight. Once you reach your total number of turns, look for a fun activity that you could do nearby, within half a mile or so. Pick a restaurant, bowling alley, gas station, movie theater, mini-golf course, park, or something else fun to explore. Make sure to have fun as you do. The goal is to do something new or unexpected.

KEY COLLECTION ZONE

What ideas resonated with you most from this section? Use this space to record after your first reading and leave space to return and add keys you find as you continue your journey. These could be words to remember, ideas to revisit, or practical steps to take that apply these concepts.

CREATIVITY KEY

_____

_____

CREATIVITY KEY

_____

_____

CREATIVITY KEY

_____

_____

CREATIVITY GUIDE CORNER – You Don't Have to Grow Up
Personal reflections to consider. Follow @one.step.guides on social media for more.

The specific environments and activities that help you experience childlikeness and express your creativity with these qualities will be unique to you. It might be via dad jokes and chuckles (like me), chasing a wondrous sunset, making time to play sports or games, or through intentional practices of generosity and kindness. Whether you are drawn to epic landscapes, unique food combinations, immersive art, or the mechanics of machines or systems, experiences of awe remind us of creative goodness and potential.

Recently I was asked about what experiences have been the most impactful during the past few years that included getting sober, shifting my career, starting a nonprofit, writing books, and undergoing a huge shift in core values and priorities. What came to mind were experiences of connection on multiple levels that restored childlikeness. Some I found in heart-alive experiences making music, or trying out new artistic expressions. Others came in moments of grace and spiritual connection, and working through past pain with a counselor. Tangible experiences of joy and love made space to look inside, process pain, grow, see beauty again, laugh, and feel permission to not have it all together. There are a lot of pressing, important challenges in the world today. You might be facing significant hurdles or needs in your own family or community. In the midst of these serious realities, carving out space for childlike moments and perspectives will help fuel your creative responses.

Chapter 10
NARRATIVE

There is more to be discovered about yourself and yorur expressions than you can see right now. Learn how to reframe weaknesses as strengths or needs and rewrite your own story in ways that fuel hope and growth.

KEY CONCEPTS
Creativity Unlocked - Chapter 10

Upgrading the Stories You Embrace

What are the narratives shaping your experience of creativity? Have you found yourself in echo chambers that dictate how you see parts of yourself and your expressions? How we view ourselves, our circumstances, and our creative potential is heavily influenced by external information that may or may not be true. We can be prone to confirmation bias that sustains self-limiting narratives when we overemphasis ideas from work, school, or home simply because they are most accessible or familiar. Our past and present experiences have conveyed thoughts that shape the stories we believe. Some are correct and helpful, while others are not and hinder our creativity. Whether an idea is objectively true or not, it can still powerfully shape our experiences. What we do with the information that enters our minds is crucial.

The stories we believe about ourselves are not permanent. In fact, our ability to rewrite these narratives is a core aspect of our creative potential. Healthy and clear vision about one aspect of our lives doesn't eliminate the potential for missing something in another. We may be only seeing a portion of the picture, and thus find ourselves unnecessarily frustrated or disappointed, harried or complacent. Think about the new ideas and expressions that you have uncovered through this book already. There is more that can be re-understood.

Your narrative holds the potential for more hope than you might see right now. The problems you have encountered are not insurmountable barriers to a life of purpose and joy. What if they instead indicate that you are designed to overcome adversity? Author Joseph Campbell famously studied and articulated the hero's journey. This is a framework for narrative extremely common in mythology that shapes many storylines in entertainment today. Fictional pieces with this structure resonate deeply with audiences because they are parallel to the human experience. Whether crafted by Shakespeare or Disney, every hero faces challenges and goes on a journey of discovery that involves friends and foes, ups and downs, mentors and mystery. Who they become through their adventures is as important as what they accomplish, and in each story there is a rejection of an old narrative in order to embrace the new.

Pick a problem that you have faced in your life. Can you see where it may indicate possibilities for your own heroic potential? There are heart-alive, creative adventures waiting for you, and what you discover can naturally provide opportunities to serve others. The narrative that sees you as a hero on a journey is as true as any lens through which you have seen yourself previously. Just because you haven't found this framing yet doesn't make it false. If you have been seeking deeper meaning or joy, there may be a new and better story to embrace. Rewriting narratives about your life can benefit your creativity by giving purpose to pain, provoking exploration, or solidifying your strengths and sources of inspiration. In his book *Social Intelligence*, clinical psychologist Dr. Daniel Goleman quotes other researchers in explaining how one can intentionally alter the story that has been created about their past:

Whenever we retrieve a memory, the brain rewrites it a bit, updating the past according to our present concerns and understanding. At the cellular level, LeDoux explains, retrieving a memory means it will be "reconsolidated," slightly altered chemically by a new protein synthesis that will help store it anew after being updated. Thus each time we bring a memory to mind, we adjust its very chemistry...*

There are new ways to understand yourself and your expressions. The narratives surrounding moments of your life and experiences of creativity could shift and become supportive of your goals. Weaknesses become opportunities for growth, problems become invitations for innovation, pain indicates a need for healing. What if the challenges you have experienced aren't just something to survive but the dragons you're meant to slay, the wounds you are made to heal, the mines from which you're meant to bring out treasure?

One Thought at a Time

Neuroscientist Dr. Mark Noble describes how recognizing and choosing new thoughts can actually be a simple but powerful form of "microneurosurgery" that transforms not only your thinking but also your feelings: "Neuronal networks are also the physical units that underlie your thoughts, feelings, and behaviors, and they change whenever you learn something new... Whenever you learn, you are modifying groups of nerve cells that work in a coordinated manner... In learning you've reached into your own brain and conducted microneurosurgery— modifying specific networks in your brain."**

A helpful tool for this reframing process is to discover the strengths or needs hidden within weaknesses. Places where we have failed or made mistakes indicate a strength overextended or a valid need that has gone unmet. For instance, being perfectionistic can actually reveal a gift for excellence or attention to detail that is over-extended. It can also indicate a need for compassion and healthier connection with ourselves or others. Co-dependency or caring too much about what others think is often taking empathy or self-awareness too far. Unhealthy coping mechanisms often indicate a valid need for rest or connection that has gone unmet.

There are more hope-filled, life-giving perspectives about yourself and your creativity waiting to be discovered. A community, mentor, coach, therapist, or counselor who cares about you and is willing to provide honest feedback can be helpful for building new narratives. Blindly embracing an optimistic viewpoint completely detached from reality can be counterproductive, as can maintaining narratives rooted solely in pain, shame, or punishment. Growth is found in the tension between the aspirational and the actual. An honest narrative does not have to be detached from difficulties or be overly dour. Opening up to trusted supporters can create space to reconsider the stories you believe about yourself, your past, and your potential. Previously unseen arrays of creative possibilities can unlock in this process, both for practical expressions and for a broader life vision that involves more childlikeness, purpose, and joy.

*Source: Daniel Goleman, Social Intelligence: The New Science of Human Relationships (London: Arrow, 2007).
**Source: Mark Noble, "TEAM CBT and the Art of Micro-Neurosurgery: A Brain User's Guide to Feeling Great," in Feeling Great: The Revolutionary New Treatment for Depression and Anxiety, ed. David Burns (Eau Claire, WI: PESI Publishing & Media, 2020), p 429-430.

JOURNAL PROMPT
Creativity Unlocked - Chapter 10

REFRAMING YOUR NARRATIVE

Think of one aspect of your story or your creative expression that has been narrated by a negative voice. It could be regret, shame, disappointment, or something else. Choose a specific, bite-sized fragment, preferably around a one-time event or a situation that took no more than a few weeks. This is an exercise to practice using your creativity to reshape your narrative, so don't pick a part of your story that's too complicated or feels overwhelming. Reflect upon and write out answers to the following questions. There are example answers in italics.

- What moment are you choosing to reframe? *Ex. Disappointment in failing an audition*

- How is the narrative you are hearing about yourself or others in the story limiting hope or leading to negative emotional experiences? *Ex. My voice isn't enough; I'm not good enough*

- What weaknesses have you previously seen in yourself when recalling this story? Are they related to one situation or part of a pattern? *Ex: I don't like my speaking voice in general*

- How can you reframe this story? Is there an overextended strength that led to this moment, or a legitimate need that you can recognize? *Ex: Artistry is a strength; need for comfort after risk*

- What positive attribute or intention can you identify behind decisions as you look at yourself from a perspective of self-compassion? *Ex: I was brave to try, and my voice is unique*

- Are there any other redemptive possibilities that you can find about yourself or others in this story? With whom could you share this reframing experience? *Ex: My friend or voice coach*

If you get stuck, feel free to take a break and come back. Experiences of fun and creative expression can help refresh and lighten the load in the midst of revisiting moments for reframing. This exercise is designed to help you explore and practice these concepts. For some situations, you might find it beneficial to get outside input from a coach, counselor, or supportive friend, if available. Once you find a reframing that brings you hope, try repeating this process for other examples of failures or weaknesses.

ACTIVATION EXERCISE
Creativity Unlocked - Chapter 10

YOUR STORY AS INSPIRATION

It's time to take a tangible step that reinforces a new, positive narrative. These are important for solidifying a new perspective. Activate your creativity via an expression that connects to your story more broadly or to the specific moment you picked for the journal activation. You can pick one of the examples below or design your own.

- Make a piece of visual art - crayons or stick figures are welcome - that captures a shift of perspective in your story.
- Write a song about your reflections or discoveries.
- Sign up for a class that past pain or failure would have discouraged.
- Brainstorm for a program or organization that could help others with similar experiences.
- Take or organize photos that inspire gratitude for important relationships.
- Revisit personal goal statements, core values, and aspirations.
- Watch a movie, listen to a podcast, or read a book about an individual whose own hero's journey inspires you.

Give yourself permission to explore this activation at your own pace. Take your next step to start now, but don't feel pressure to finish today. This might look like starting a project, telling a friend your new goal, or preparing materials or time to create.

BONUS: PEAKS AND VALLEYS

Not every season is going to feel like you're winning, in your creativity or your life more broadly. It can be helpful to recognize that the process can be full of ups and downs, just like the path of a hike or a mountain ridge. Recognizing existing high points can help encourage us when we're in a challenging season. Using the image below, or by drawing your own, label a few high points with key moments or progress steps you've made. They don't have to be in order. If it helps your process, you can also label low points, and celebrate that you're still moving forward.

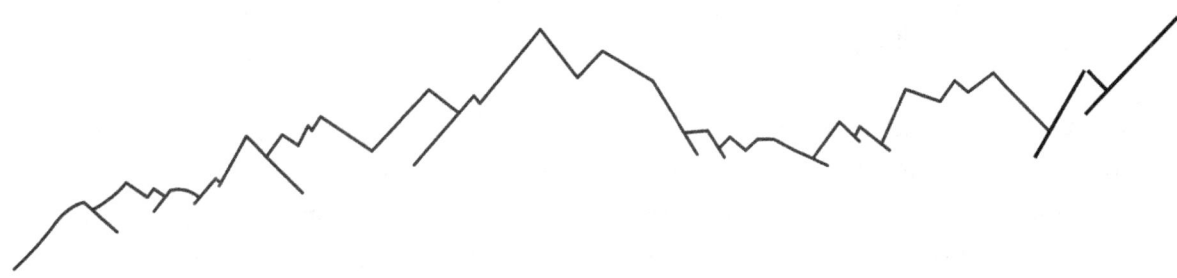

KEY COLLECTION ZONE

What ideas resonated with you most from this section? Use this space to record after your first reading and leave space to return and add keys you find as you continue your journey. These could be words to remember, ideas to revisit, or practical steps to take that apply these concepts.

CREATIVITY KEY

CREATIVITY KEY

CREATIVITY KEY

CREATIVITY GUIDE CORNER - You Can Rewrite Your Story

Personal reflections to consider. Follow @one.step.growth on social media for more.

Neither the positive nor the negative aspects of your past define your story. What you've tried and failed. The messes you've made. The battles you've won and those you have lost. Your accomplishments. Your missed opportunities. The people you've loved or hurt. None of these ultimately define your value as a person imbued with the gift of creativity. You are a human being worthy of love. Whether you express through finger taps, fountain pens, or Philly cheesesteaks, your story is still being written. I didn't realize how much my own creativity was sabotaged for years by an understandable but overly negative narrative about myself and the world around me. My worst failures layered shame on me that sapped courage. I struggled to embrace goodness and love. Working with a counselor and a coach helped me identify how toxic narratives had started forming at an early age and kept me on a knife's edge of pressure. Experiences of comfort and vulnerable connection with others helped me rewrite my story, take action when needed, and move forward.

There's a version of your story better than you've heard thus far. The obstacles you've faced or are facing now will not be what defines your journey. No, it is your heart, your courage, your willingness to go deeper in vulnerability and connection, in appropriate settings, that can fuel the adventures of your life. Life is short. Our bodies go from dust to dust. But in between we can experience creative beauty and goodness that make us come alive.

Chapter 11
REDEMPTION

Do you get discouraged by disruptions to your plans or mistakes? Within mess awaits meaningful and powerful ingredients for your expressions. Discover a step-by-step approach to redemptive creativity.

KEY CONCEPTS
Creativity Unlocked – Chapter 11

Finding Hidden Treasure

There is creative fuel waiting to be discovered in what has been messy or imperfect in your life. Within both daily routines and dream projects, there are opportunities to turn the crap you experience into fertilizer for expressions that can grow unexpectedly sweet and nourishing fruit. In the moment, the messes may not carry anything you want to smell, let alone utilize. But the right tools and approach can help you find hidden treasures. Whether the mess is your own fault, accidental, or someone else's, difficulties can trigger life-giving moments that spark meaningful and impactful creative outflows.

Past experiences that were sour or sweet can serve as inspiration or motivation. Much of the art we consume comes out of the heartbreak, anger, or loss that their creators have experienced, whether directly or indirectly. From poet Maya Angelou to author J.R.R. Tolkien to world leader Nelson Mandela, difficulty has inspired powerful and beautiful expressions. This principle is true for both the minor inconveniences and the major difficulties that shape your everyday experiences. Whether a spat with friends or broken family relationships, a short-term sickness or major health limitations, a missed opportunity for fun or a permanent loss, there is creative value to uncover. Problems you face every day can offer the chance to bring about a solution and experience the joy and satisfaction that creative cognition activates. Here are five types of unexpected treasures that adversity can spark. It can be helpful to begin exploring these concepts with less intense experiences of mess, and grow from there.

- *Empathy.* Challenges can fuel compassion for people with similar experiences.
- *Meaningful connection.* Opportunities to be compassionate or real with yourself or others can arise in processing the pain of difficulty, seeking shifts, or pursuing solutions.
- *Learning.* Problems offer opportunities to discover a new way of doing things, whether via a different choice, approach, skill set, or product.
- *Expertise.* The knowledge you gain can develop into future creative expressions with greater authoritative insight and understanding of others' experiences.
- *Inspiration and motivation.* Necessity is the mother of invention. The pain you're feeling can inspire action, complex and powerful art, or a whole range of practical solutions.

These benefits don't eliminate the reality of difficulties. This is not about stuffing down negative emotions or pretending they don't exist. You probably won't want to linger in the messy discomfort of failures. But, as you start to recognize and experience unexpected benefits hidden within hard situations, hope for present and future difficulties can increase. It's possible to actually build patterns of anticipating something good and naturally start looking for creative ideas. You still may need to process through the pain. But, new thoughts and tangible actions can shift your experiences in a redemptive way that translates into practical and life-giving creativity. There is nothing off-limits from serving as fuel for your expressions.

JOURNAL PROMPT
Creativity Unlocked - Chapter 11

STRENGTHENING REDEMPTIVE MINDSETS

Upgrading mindsets can help you experience more of the benefits of redemptive creativity. As you consider opportunities for reframing, are there areas that feel difficult or even impossible to find redemptive possibilities? There could be viewpoints about certain situations formed through past pain that limit your discovery of something new. Look for contexts that lead you to say or think "It's always....." "This is just how it is......" "It's hopeless.....". Taking small steps to start recognizing and upgrading these mindsets can unlock new opportunities for redemptive creativity. It's important that you feel permission to go at your own pace with this. Here are a few examples of affirmations focused on giving yourself permission to see something new.

- "I let go of my old perspective of _____ and I welcome opportunities to discover _____ through the process.

- "I give myself permission to explore a new understanding of _____, even though it has held experiences of pain, confusion, or uncertainty in the past."

- "My thoughts and feelings are not permanent, and I choose to embrace new perspectives and my power to choose them."

Use the lines below and keys in the section on mindsets to make your own affirmations. Return to this exercise as many times as you need to. As you practice creative reframing and see its fruit in your life, the more you'll begin to see the value and possibility of these tools.

NEW REDEMPTIVE CREATIVITY AFFIRMATIONS

1. _____

2. _____

3. _____

JOURNAL PROMPT
Creativity Unlocked – Chapter 11

DAILY REFRAMING BRAINSTORM

A little bit of reflection can help us identify the hidden treasures of inspiration and connection in the midst of our daily difficulties. Let's brainstorm how we can apply the concept of creative reframing to our regular schedules. Use the space below or another sheet of paper to reflect upon the following questions:

- What regular activities or responsibilities in your life could use reframing? List out a few current settings that feel exhausting, monotonous, or otherwise unpleasant within family routines, work, artistic expressions, or other parts of life.
- Where can you see potential for these experiences to hold meaningful connection or inspiration for expressions? Are there opportunities for learning, expertise, or empathy? It's okay if you don't have answers for every area, discovery can take time.
- Now, revisit your Resonance Map and your list of creative themes and activities from earlier chapters. Can you see ways to bring interests or skills that bring you personal joy or meaning into some of these mundane or difficult moments?

Examples of Difficulty Fueling Creative Opportunity
- *Running errands becomes space for connection with loved ones via the phone or a creative moment to enjoy your favorite science podcast or pop music*
- *Sad events invite connection with others, motivation to meet a need, or artistic inspiration*
- *Challenges at work spark development of a new solution or an honest conversation with colleagues or leadership about the problems or your career direction*
- *Missing appointments or transportation can spark chance meetings or new vantage points*

ACTIVATION EXERCISE
Creativity Unlocked – Chapter 11

RECLAIM THE MUNDANE AND DIFFICULT MOMENTS

Now that we have a list of opportunities for reframing, it's time to experiment with turning less-than-glamorous parts of life into moments of creating joy or connection. Use your answers from the previous pages to activate a redemptive activity today. Spend at least 15 minutes on it. Make a call, write the song, brainstorm a solution, read or listen to inspiring content, meet up with a friend, or find connection, inspiration, or learning in another way. You could also consider how a longer-term difficulty has prepared you to express yourself in ways that are personally meaningful, whether via volunteering with an organization, making art that relates, or simply having a conversation with a friend going through a similar situation.

If not possible to fully activate your ideas today, prepare for your next opportunity. For instance, look for a book or knitting project for future surprise delays. Research a new class or explore podcasts you would want to listen when you do the dishes or clean your house. Revisit your passion and "why" for your job. Is it helping fund other goals, for yourself or your loved ones? Plan extra time for your trip so you can stop at your favorite view or coffee shop, or schedule a window this week to drive an extra few miles to catch a sunset. Buy a journal or sketchbook so that you can doodle or take note of artistic or innovative inspiration that sparks from challenges. Resonance Map in your phone and use it collect ideas. Talking with a friend, watching DIY videos, or checking out Pinterest can also be helpful for brainstorming.

Try to pick something memorable that brings you joy. The goal is to start building patterns of recognizing creative opportunity. Use the lines below to describe your experience, or your plan, and check the box when complete.

REDEMPTIVE CREATIVITY ACTIVITY PLAN

_____

_____

_____

_____

Check this box when you have completed your activity.

ACTIVATION EXERCISE
Creativity Unlocked – Chapter 11

RECLAIM MUNDANE AND DIFFICULT MOMENTS

Hidden within the storms of life are opportunities for meaningful connection, learning, and more via creativity. Use the lines to label each cloud below with a situation or responsibility that feels most mundane or unpleasant. Then, start filling in ideas for creative redemption on the clouds themselves, whether via inspiration, expertise, empathy, or something else. Bonus points if you use colorful ink or paste in images as you creatively "reclaim" these cloudy spots.

KEY COLLECTION ZONE

What ideas resonated with you most from this section? Use this space to record after your first reading and leave space to return and add keys you find as you continue your journey. These could be words to remember, ideas to revisit, or practical steps to take that apply these concepts.

CREATIVITY KEY

CREATIVITY KEY

CREATIVITY KEY

 **CREATIVITY GUIDE CORNER – Mining Treasures from Mess**
Personal reflections to consider. Follow @one.step.growth on social media for more.

Opportunities for creative reframing and inspiration are all around us. A tough week in my first year of sobriety inspired resonant characters and themes for a writing project. Arriving at a wedding on the wrong day serendipitously sparked a new long-term friendship. Gaps in recovery resources fueled creation of a new nonprofit. A poor late night decision inspired a new song. Supporting a team member's bittersweet move made room for a new colleague whose skillset was perfect for a documentary that we didn't know we would be filming. Challenges, difficulty, or even mistakes can be the birthplace of great creativity.

The more that we can celebrate these redemptive moments, the easier they are to identify as we move forward. It's still important to process pain, disappointment, or frustration, even as we look for creative opportunities. Experiencing connection and knowing that we're not alone in hard moments can help fuel these discoveries. There is redemptive purpose and even joy that can flow out of experiences for which that seems impossible now. Creativity is a superpower that becomes especially visible when it bumps into messy, disappointing parts of life. When a plan falls through or you experience rejection, what could you create with that time? How could major difficulties or minor speed bumps lead to unexpected discoveries? Finding this treasure via experimenting in small messes will build courage to believe for redemptive possibilities in bigger challenges.

Chapter 12
REFINEMENT

Refresh expressions that have become stale by pursuing excellence. Upgrade experiences of feedback with an approach that honors your heart and voice. Celebrating growth will fuel new discoveries.

KEY CONCEPTS
Creativity Unlocked – Chapter 12

A Natural Progression

Your ongoing steps to increase joy and connection in your creativity can naturally fuel refinement of your craft. It's normal to want the best for something you care about. Loving your creativity often motivates growth. Feedback can help you explore and increase the quality and delight that your creativity provides, first as a gift to yourself and then as a natural overflow that impacts others. It can be rewarding to experience greater excellence or effectiveness.

Refinement helps expressions remain meaningful and fresh over time. Sometimes creative activities start to feel stale because change or growth is needed. The delight of bringing something new into existence can decrease when it becomes no longer new in some way. Think of a baby: there is sheer joy found in learning to walk or speak, or witnessing these incredible moments. But these poignant discoveries are not designed to simply stay in that initial state. We don't typically find great significance in a teenager saying a word or taking a step unless there is a special circumstance. Breakthroughs as a baby or toddler are the building blocks for more complex experiences that provide continued joy and satisfaction. Initial expressions of movement and communication provide the pathway to new skills that require learning and feedback, whether racing dirt bikes, crafting arguments in speeches, or building a home. Refinement will take your expressions to places far beyond what you can see now.

What's one expression that brings you intrinsic joy? Chances are there has already been development of skill or a new context that helps keep it interesting and rewarding. The law of diminishing returns applies to our creativity: staying in a similar place or level may not provide the same delight or meaning forever. But there is a natural creative progression, rooted in love and not in pressure, that can continually fuel joy through growth. A plateau or stale season is not failure; it's an opportunity for discovery. These moments can become a vehicle for deepening connection with your own creative identity, with others, and with something greater.

The seasoning of someone else's wisdom or skills can refresh your creativity. Asking people for input and investing in your craft will help you better translate your creativity into experiences that people can access or digest. Whether or not you share your expressions with others, there is an intrinsic value in the process of engaging with feedback and deepening excellence and expertise (there may be practical, financial benefits too). Many a gifting goes under-appreciated or under-developed due to missed opportunities to refine or modify the expression. Part of the satisfaction of refinement comes from unlocking new possibilities. If you have been waiting for an opportunity to open up or have not seen the doors open that you desire, you might need to seek feedback and invest time in developing your expression further. A fear of critique or the growth process keeps many from both experiencing fresh joy and connection around their creativity and accomplishing goals in their careers, their hobbies, and personal lives.

Navigating the Tensions in Feedback and Growth

However, the process of refinement can bring up external considerations that may feel in conflict with the priorities of personal joy that you have been activating through this workbook. This tension is not your enemy. It's an opportunity to discover how you personally will weigh important internal and external considerations. The greater the confidence in your creative identity, the more freedom you will feel in considering others' ideas or incorporating change in your expressions without losing your voice and satisfaction. You can develop an approach to refinement that fits your specific goals and needs, and you don't have to do it alone.

Intentionally pursuing feedback for your expressions also provides opportunity to strengthen your own belief systems and community. Constructive feedback can be tough to receive, but it provides an opportunity for us to revisit our roots: our own inherent value and beauty, not needing perfection or someone else's validation. Inviting and implementing feedback can be humbling. Remember: though others' perspectives can be incredibly helpful gifts, your worth and creative potential aren't based on their opinions. Constructive feedback does not change the value or significance of your creative outflows, whether in art, work, or other forms.

Pruning is a powerful and important part of the creative process. Many expressions benefit from some form of the concept "less is more." At times you will need to focus on certain activities, commitments, or ideas and let go of good things. Perspectives from others can be incredibly helpful in this process, because familiarity can cloud our vision. But, beauty and excellence remain in the eye of the beholder. Getting input does not have to trump the creative idea you envision. Suggestions of what could be improved or cut out can be helpful, but they are not authoritative truth. Difference of opinion or disagreement does not have to undermine your significance or authority as a creative being. There is a difference between subjective taste and objective truth. Most expressions benefit from helpful, basic feedback that is more objective, like if a beat isn't consistently in rhythm or the vocals are out of tune in a song. Other pieces of input will be far more subjective, and should be evaluated.

When you receive feedback, whether or not it was sought, reflect on which pieces might be more objectively helpful and if there are components based on that person's taste. Scour the ideas shared for any wisdom you can glean, even if a lot of the feedback doesn't resonate. If unsure, get a second, third, or hundredth opinion. As you reflect, you will find ideas that are either immediately helpful, best to explore later, or something you should politely dump. You don't have to tell the person that you're disregarding those pieces.

Developing healthy refinement practices can feel a bit like eating one's less tasty vegetables or implementing a new exercise regimen. It's not always fun. But these short-term, uncomfortable moments will help you maintain and increase the joy and meaning in your expressions. Each instance requires holding something good with an open hand and being willing to let it evolve. What has been good for a previous season may actually be part of the pathway to something greater. Your past and present creative outputs can serve future expression in surprising ways.

JOURNAL PROMPT
Creativity Unlocked - Chapter 12

SMALL STEPS TOWARD GROWTH

Each of us are in different places with refining or improving our creative expressions. Grab your journal or use the space on the next page to complete the steps below. The goal of this journaling exercise is to identify personal, tangible, and achievable steps for your current refinement needs, inspired by the well-known SMART-method. SMART is an acronym that stands for Specific, Measurable, Attainable, Relevant and Time-Bound.*

- **Step one:** Jot down at least five creative themes or activities that bring you intrinsic joy or satisfaction. Remember, they could be in the arts, in experiences, in work, or in other formats. There is no need to overanalyze them or depict them in perfect language.

- **Step two:** Next to each, write one or two personal goals you have for this expression. Examples could be: "enjoy myself + exercise" for nature hikes, "perform at an open-mic night" for standup comedy, "turn this hobby into a career" for a class you teach, "make a five course meal" for cooking, "get your book published" for writing, and "use time to learn something new" for your commute to work.

- **Step three:** Identify the next step toward refinement that you can take to improve your process or progress toward this larger goal or experience. Make this a mini-goal. For instance, "discover a new hiking location," "ask a friend for input on comedy routine," "find educational podcast" or "practice recipes for new dishes." Some of the most helpful steps can be identifying an individual, resource, or community that can help you move forward.

- **Step four:** Take a look at the specific goals you've written down and adjust to make sure they are achievable. You may also want to scale back as you experiment, where necessary. For instance, you could dial back to "ask a friend for hiking spot tips," "self-edit your comedy routine draft," or "buy groceries for new recipes." If you find yourself not making the progress you want, return to this exercise and pick a smaller next step that you can identify.

- **Step five:** Pick one or two of these mini-goals to prioritize. Give them a specific deadline or timeframe. For instance, "I'll make a new appetizer or salad by Wednesday" or "I'll spend two hours on writing in the next two days." Use the lines on the next page to complete the exercise. Feel free to modify to meet your needs.

*Source: Doran, G. T. (1981). "There's a S.M.A.R.T. Way to Write Management's Goals and Objectives", Management Review, Vol. 70, Issue 11, pp. 35-36.

JOURNAL PROMPT
Creativity Unlocked - Chapter 12

SMALL STEPS TOWARD GROWTH

Use the lines below to complete the steps on the previous page. The goal of this exercise is to help you build experience for ongoing and future refinement of your expressions. Some expressions may require more tangible feedback from people while others will simply benefit from self-reflection. A significant factor for making continued progress in growth and refinement is recognizing how internal thoughts and emotions affect us. If you find yourself stuck and aren't sure why, explore tools from earlier sections on healing and mindsets.

ACTIVATION EXERCISE
Creativity Unlocked - Chapter 12

USING REFINEMENT KEYS

On this page and the next, there are five practical keys for refining creative expressions. Read through all of them first and then circle at least two of the five that you need to implement in expressions that you highlighted in the journal exercise. Then, follow the action instructions. Make time over the next week to apply these keys. Start at least one action step today.

Refinement Key 1: Embrace pauses and pace adjustments for expressions.

Action: Pick one project or creative expression that feels stagnant and choose to put it aside for a month. Replace it with a different life-giving activity, and start experimenting more with that creative outlet. Take note of where you find resonance in the new expression.

Refinement Key 2: Invite feedback from trusted sources.

Action: Send an unfinished creative project to two or three individuals that could help you refine it. First ask if they have capacity to help and then send specific questions and requests for what you need in your current phase. Be detailed about what you're needing.

Refinement Key 3: Revisit input for fresh exploration.

Action: Find a piece of feedback that someone has given you that hasn't previously been fully applied. Read or listen to it again and identify the key elements. What parts could help your project? Are there any ideas from the feedback with which you could experiment? Try out a new idea, as long you're comfortable with its effect (or have a way to undo the change).

ACTIVATION EXERCISE
Creativity Unlocked - Chapter 12

REFINEMENT IS KEY

Refinement Key 4: Learn from others more skilled than you.

Action Option 1: Ask a friend who's more experienced in the creative expression if you can shadow them for a day or join a group or community they are involved with.

Action Option 2: Email an expert you admire with some specific questions. You'd be surprised how many well-known people will take the time to respond, when presented with a reasonable request in a humble, grateful way. Even if they don't, celebrate the step you've taken.

Action Option 3: Search online for a free video instructional for your expression. Watch it and take notes of ideas and tips that resonate with your journey.

Refinement Key 5: Commit to investing in your growth.

Action Option 1: Find and commit to a local workshop or online course. Reserve the dates in your calendar, sign up, or take other concrete actions. Check out onestepgrowth.com for details on our Creativity Unlocked and Creativity Activated groups.

Action Option 2: Research what tools or gear, whether digital or tangible, would benefit your creative expression and how much they cost. Cut one small weekly expense and set it aside to save up for this purchase.

KEY COLLECTION ZONE

What ideas resonated with you most from this section? Use this space to record after your first reading and leave space to return and add keys you find as you continue your journey. These could be words to remember, ideas to revisit, or practical steps to take that apply these concepts.

CREATIVITY KEY

CREATIVITY KEY

CREATIVITY KEY

CREATIVITY GUIDE CORNER - From Plateaus to Platforms
Personal reflections to consider. Follow @one.step.growth on social media for more.

I used to feel stymied by stale moments or experience shame in getting stuck because I interpreted them through a lens of failure. Uncertainty and fear increased when an expression in my work or art lost its luster. When a writing project paused or the meaningful volunteer experience provided less joy, I would feel deflated or worried. Today, I have learned to embrace these moments as opportunities for rest and ongoing growth. They are part of the natural progression creativity is meant to have to keep it fresh.

Do you find it hard to receive feedback? A significant part of growth is intentionally pursuing input, and learning how to filter and glean from what is shared while staying true to your authentic voice and passions. I recently showed up for a coffee with a potential collaborator full of enthusiasm. After a positive start, the person shared a constructive thought that made my heart sink, especially because it was unexpected. But after I sat with the idea, I could see that there were some elements I needed to hear and other pieces I could drop. It wasn't comfortable, but it was valuable. Over the years, I've become more intentional about from whom, how, and when I seek input. Practice has helped me get more specific, build confidence, overcome old voices of insecurity, and share ideas with others in better ways. Now, I see the vulnerability of giving or receiving feedback as the cost of a gift. Both parties are risking misperception or disconnection to offer something potentially valuable.

Chapter 13
AUDIENCE

Sharing your creativity with others, in any form, can be risky and rewarding. Loving your expressions often naturally leads to more visibility, so it's important to learn how to sustainability navigate creating with an audience.

KEY CONCEPTS
Creativity Unlocked – Chapter 13

The Joys and Costs of Visibility

Creative expressions are like plants or trees that, watered by delight and connection, will grow in height and fruitfulness. Visibility will increase. Branches will naturally develop fruit or cones that offer sustenance and joy for audiences. Whether in developing your skills at work, hosting parties, painting landscapes, or volunteering at a school, your growth in expressions you love will attract eyes and ears. They will also offer new benefit to others. At times this greater exposure will stem from your choice, and in other moments it will be outside of your control. The process can involve new external challenges, like winds, that test your foundational roots.

Sharing one's creative expressions with people can spark powerful emotions. There may be a mixture of excitement, hope, anxiety, concern, fear, or adrenaline-fueled delight. Having others partake of your expressions holds risks and rewards. It is gratifying to see an audience enjoy or benefit from what you have brought forth. But the process can also be painful. There can be experiences of misperception or rejection. A journey to discover one's audiences is common. They often are not clear right away, and they could include colleagues, neighbors, family members, followers, or certain groups of people most drawn to your expressions. The foundations of personal joy, intrinsic meaning, and connection you're developing will help you navigate this exploration. There is a pathway discoverable between two unhelpful extremes: being paralyzed by fear, and oversharing out of a need for approval. Prioritizing connection with your own heart helps, as it provides an automatic reward no matter the response from others. It also increases the likelihood of it inspiring audiences. They can sense and are drawn to the vulnerability of authentic expression, which is the gift you are choosing to give.

Remember that the process of sharing your expressions or having a specific response does not make you a more valuable human being. Similarly, keeping things personal or unseen does not make you less valuable. Both types of experiences can be fun and fulfilling, or dissatisfying or unenjoyable, depending on the approach and timing. The evolving context of your life will influence how, when, and what to share. This includes both your personal growth and the environments in which you find yourself. There may be whole channels and future audiences beyond what seems possible or likely now. Learning how to navigate sharing expressions is not a one-time process. As you experiment, continue to replace negative comparison with positive thoughts, celebrate your victories, and resist perfectionism.

Sharing your creativity is not a race. Give yourself time to pause or rest, especially after taking uncomfortable steps forward. Remember that vulnerability sparks the deeper connection that can fuel more fulfilling experiences of life. The important thing is to maintain connection as you keep progressing. It's possible to learn to enjoy the process of sharing more.

JOURNAL PROMPT
Creativity Unlocked – Chapter 13

"TIP"-TOEING FORWARD IN YOUR SHARING

We have compiled five tips for navigating sharing creative expressions with an audience, whether you're inviting someone on a trip, posting on social media, or presenting an artistic or work project. Take a moment to answer the questions. If they resonate, you might want to journal out more ideas on how you can apply the tip to a creative expression. You can use different activities, and you may not have answers for all right now.

TIP 1: Recognize Your Motivations and Capacity. Unexpressed and unmet expectations in sharing creativity are a common source of pain and disappointment that get people stuck. What are your goals, really, for taking a next step of sharing with an audience? If the response is not what you hope for, do you have capacity to deal with disappointment?

TIP 2: Take a Staged Approach that Honors Your Capacity. A baby steps approach to the process of sharing will fuel your journey over the long haul and ultimately make you unstoppable. Consider your context and emotional capacity. Where do you need to slow down and take a smaller step? Or, where could reducing your goals help you move forward?

TIP 3: Develop Strength by Stepping Into Opportunities for Rejection. There will be moments of sharing your creativity with external audiences when the next healthy steps feel uncertain and uncomfortable because rejection is possible. The post may not get likes, the person may not respond, the audience may not make purchases. These moments are opportunities for growth in strength and resilience. Where do you have capacity to take a risk in sharing your creative expressions that might lead to a disappointing response? How will you handle the emotions that arise? Who can remind you that rejection is not failure, or the end?

TIP 4: Embrace the Vulnerability of Sharing as an Act of Generosity. The uncertainty in sharing creativity with others is a cost of the beautiful gift you give to your audience. Approach the possibility of rejection and other doubts you might face as part of the price you pay to offer others an opportunity for insight, beauty, or connection. This framing can help you move forward when you're stuck, as it gives discomfort a sense of purpose. Where do you need to reframe the process of sharing an expression? Reflect on potential negative experiences (the "costs") of sharing and what is to be gained (the "benefits")..

TIP 5: Adjust Your Measurement System. Be intentional about defining success when you share and be open to it changing. Your initial goal of impacting others might shift to self-learning. Financial and other tangible rewards might appear as goals around something you started sharing for personal joy. Recognize and celebrate the external and internal metrics that matter for you in your given season. Remember that you can only do so much to influence peoples' responses. For which expressions do you need to intentionally revisit your definition of success? How can that help you move forward in your journey?

ACTIVATION EXERCISE
Creativity Unlocked - Chapter 13

THE GIFT OF VULNERABILITY

Let's activate the reframing of sharing a creative expressions as a generous gift. You can walk through it step by step. Pull out a pen and separate piece of paper so that you can capture your thoughts and follow the instructions below. While this exercise includes journaling, it is designed to be an activation, so make sure to complete every step for the full experience.

- Pick an area of your creative expressions or personal growth where you want to increase in confidence and ability to share with others. Write this on the page.

- Next, list out three or four different ways that you could share this expression with an "audience" in different stages of your journey. This could be telling a friend, talking about it with a counselor or mentor, inviting someone to a showing or event, posting on social media, or presenting a version of your expression in real life at work, home, or at an event. Some ideas might be new and others can be actions you have already taken. Brainstorming these possibilities for one expression will help you develop steps for others in the future.

- Reflect for a few minutes. In what ways would sharing the gift of your expression create value or connection for the recipient via these different steps? This could be through a moment of shared understanding and empathy, relational connection, a story that inspires, knowledge or tools that solve a problem, an experience of community, a moment of wonder or beauty that refreshes one's soul, a clearer sense of direction, or something else.

- Now, pick one act of sharing to try this week. It can be one that you have taken before, but want to try again, or something new. Before you do, remind yourself of your personal definition of success for this step. Reflect on the possible gifts you are seeking to give to others, whether or not they are received or acknowledged. Remember, the impact may be direct or indirect, seen or unseen. Sometimes the gift we end up sharing is different than what we intend. For instance, an attempt to present a lovely cake could turn into a gift of laughter and an unforgettable memory with one accidental slip. The art you share with a particular emotional style might be interpreted very differently by another.

Don't rush through the process. After you take the step of sharing you plan out, think about if there's a gift or value that you sensed the audience receiving. Whether or not they did, celebrate that you have offered them the gift, no matter their response. Want to keep growing in sharing your creativity? Repeat this next week, using another form of creative expression.

KEY COLLECTION ZONE

What ideas resonated with you most from this section? Use this space to record after your first reading and leave space to return and add keys you find as you continue your journey. These could be words to remember, ideas to revisit, or practical steps to take that apply these concepts.

CREATIVITY KEY

CREATIVITY KEY

CREATIVITY KEY

CREATIVITY GUIDE CORNER – Find Expression-Audience Fit

Personal reflections to consider. Follow @one.step.growth for more.

As someone who has experienced both pain and incredible heart-alive moments in sharing my creativity, learning to consider my capacity for vulnerability has been key. Whether I'm posting on social media, sending a book chapter for review, planning a party, or taking a romantic risk, there can be an emotional cost regardless of the outcome. We can get creatively stuck in places where we don't have capacity to process or handle the downside. Leading a storytelling nonprofit focused on recovery has deepened my appreciation for the importance of considering timing and capacity for sharing. Some days I have more or less due to my sleep, diet, exercise, or spiritual practices. My capacity for vulnerability keeps evolving. The more I focus on personal joy and meaning in what I express, the easier it is to share because audience validation is more like frosting on top of an already delicious cake. The intrinsic benefits of creativity are far more consistent than the validation of others.

In the world of start-ups, experts are constantly looking to find what's called product-market fit, meaning a value that motivates a response by an audience. Aspects of this concept can help you take your next steps around sharing. As you take small risks, you can gain understanding of who connects to what you're creating, and in what ways. The process of experimenting may feel vulnerable; stay connected to what brings you personal joy and meaning. Your creativity is not going to resonate with everyone, and that's okay!

Chapter 14
LONGEVITY

Learn how to thrive creatively over the long-haul and prevent burnout. A multi-faceted approach to creating joy & purpose is essential. Adjust pace and priorities to fuel flourishing for yourself and your loved ones.

KEY CONCEPTS
Creativity Unlocked - Chapter 14

Avoiding the Pitfalls

Newspapers and history books are littered with tragic stories displaying a hidden danger: talented artists who loved their craft but became isolated and unstable, impactful inventors who lost relationship with their children or spouse, well-intentioned social-justice or religious leaders embroiled in secret lives, successful entrepreneurs with broken families. Too many impactful creative individuals, who rightfully are honored for their contributions to society, had significant points of failure in their leadership or personal lives. Or, in a moment of great pressure, they capitulated to compromise, brought unnecessary pain to others, strayed from their values, and tarnished both their own joy and their impact on the world. Human beings are not perfect. Life is full of stumbles. But intentionally building a creative process with a focus on longevity can fuel connection and help you avoid unnecessary pain.

A word of caution: the powerful delight that creativity activates holds hidden dangers. The natural joy and passion builds momentum for expressions, strengthens emotional health, and adds purpose to daily life. However, these rewards make it possible to overindulge in particular outflows at the expense of other important priorities. Spending too much time and energy in certain aspects of creativity can negatively impact personal wellness, relationships with loved ones, and one's dream projects. Moderation is often helpful, and will help prevent unnecessary difficulties and detours. More of a specific expression is not always better. Intention around your pace and priorities will help you not burn out or run out of gas on your creative journey.

There are structures you can put in place today that reduce the chances of your pursuit of purpose and joy via creativity swallowing you whole. Think of them as maintenance routines and guardrails that will help you progress—and thrive—holistically. Adding these approaches to your journey will sustain growth and deepen delight across your multiple creative roles: as a friend, a spouse, a significant other, a parent, a leader, a colleague, or a creative collaborator. You are designed to be a releaser of solutions, beauty, and goodness in the world. If you find yourself carrying too much weight, getting lonely, afraid, or struggling with negative thoughts, please reach out for help. The world needs the light that your life represents.

Longevity isn't just playing defense. Proactively building a sustainable approach to your creativity is important for achieving goals. Meaningful, excellent creative projects can require months, years, or even decades. Whether your dreams are for now or the future, develop vision for both what you're creating and how you can navigate the journey. Reflecting on the art, career, experiences, social impact, or relationships you're building can help when the process gets tedious or when you need to make hard choices. Your wellness matters more than what you can make. There will be more projects and opportunities, but there is only one you.

Why We Overindulge

Science has shown that the human brain is wired to seek that which most easily brings pleasure or safety. When we find something that offers joy or comfort, we are prone to utilize it at an ever-increasing rate. Thus, as we unlock delightful, satisfying creativity, we can over-prioritize certain activities at the expense of other important needs. The neural pathways in our brains that provide pleasure through a particular expression, whether sculpture, skiing, or stock trading, become superhighways. Meanwhile, others that could spur joy through channels like relational connection are not firing as frequently and can become further neglected. Our brains gravitate toward the path of least resistance, and suddenly we are on the sixth episode of a bingeable TV show or the fourth hour of painting. Overindulgence has the potential to hinder needed actions tied to important responsibilities around wellness, finances, and relationships. When our brains are full of endorphins from creating, it's harder to note these deficiencies.

We are more likely to overemphasize expressions that provide comfort when other aspects of life that could provide connection or joy are unstable. For instance, it's easier to indulge too much in video games, shopping, or substances when family or friend relationships aren't life-giving. When we are having a hard time connecting with ourselves, others, or something greater, that Netflix drama, extra hours at the office, glass of wine, or bowl of ice cream becomes more appealing. We might create experiences of short-term joy via these activities but they can become addictive patterns in our brains that could lead to long-term consequences like dependency and burnout. The keys below can help you flourish emotionally, avoid overindulgence, increase longevity, and reduce the chances that you hurt yourself or others on the creative journey. You can start putting these in place today.

- **Embrace your multifaceted creative nature.** You are creating in dozens of contexts every month: via relationships, hobbies, work, service, nature trips, or other experiences. Finding meaningful connection and delight in multiple types of expressions decreases overindulgence and increases flexibility for delays and uncertainty that can arise. If key parts of your life aren't life-giving, seek help via a counselor, coach, or other resource.
- **Intentionally set your pace.** Timing is everything. Reflect on and adjust your pace and priorities as seasons change. Consider where you're finding momentum, satisfaction and joy, or where it's lacking, and whether your pace is supporting your wellness. Take note also of where you're finding connection across all three levels—self, others, and something greater. You will need, at times, to make a powerful decision to rest or put something aside when everything inside wants to rush. At other moments, you will need to bravely step into action propelled by your goals, dreams, and visions, resisting the pressure to stay stuck.
- **Set strong priorities within your creative outflows.** Not every expression needs equal attention. Too much of a good thing can be an enemy of your wellness and joy. Overloading your plate with responsibility, even around activities that bring you life, can wear you down. Practice saying a powerful "no" to opportunities will set you up for longevity, as options often increase as joy and excellence in creativity grow.
- **Implement a burnout prevention plan.** Make a list of warning signs that indicate when change is needed, like irritation, drinking or eating too much, or other coping mechanisms. Use this workbook and other tools to understand your needs and ways to address them.

JOURNAL PROMPT
Creativity Unlocked – Chapter 14

PERSONAL OVERINDULGENCE SURVEY

Write down a few real-life examples of how either unhealthy pace or overindulgence has impacted creativity or other parts of life. It doesn't have to be a big event. The subtle and small expressions of the pitfalls are actually best. Try to be as specific as you can.

_____

_____

_____

As you reflect on these instances, do you see patterns? Perhaps it's around a certain activity in which you tend to spend too much time, a specific mood or context that makes you more likely to rush, or an underlying need or desire you're trying to fill. There's no shame or judgement in recognizing these tendencies. You are simply gaining information and awareness. Use the lines below to reflect on possible patterns and steps you can take to address them. Think about tools from this workbook you can apply. Where do you need to remember an affirmation or strengthen a mindset? Is there a healthier way that you could create an experience of comfort or joy? How can you keep your connection tank filled? Pressure to move too fast or stay stuck often comes from shame or fear. Are there are experiences of community that can help reduce your desire to over-indulge? Making these questions a regular reflection will increase awreness of what helps you best.

Here's an example reflection to get you started:
I have a tendency to feel rushed when I write. Sometimes I work so hard on passion projects that I struggle to take a break. I think it comes from feeling behind or like I'm not doing enough. Some of these moments are sparked by shame. To address this pattern I'm going to daily revisit affirmations.

_____

_____

ACTIVATION EXERCISE
Creativity Unlocked – Chapter 14

ACTIVATING YOUR BURNOUT PREVENTION PLAN

It's time to take action! You can do one, two, or all of the following steps:

Share the list of "future risks for creative pitfalls" with a trusted friend or creative partner. Give them permission to call out any of these behaviors if they observe it, in kindness and with grace.

Set a reminder for 3-6 months from now to do a quick self-check to assess how you're doing. Are you maintaining a healthy pace and foundation for your creative pursuits? Are any adjustments to priorities or pace necessary to avoid burnout or rush?

Implement small changes, one step at a time, to your creative process. Set time limits for a day or week. Remind yourself of what success looks like in a given season. Reduce exposure to information, news, or people that fuel shame or pressure, or lead to overindulgence. Reflect, experiment, refine, and try again. Even if you walk back a change, you are learning to experiment and finding how to make yourself less susceptible to pitfalls.

KEY COLLECTION ZONE

What ideas resonated with you most from this section? Use this space to record after your first reading and leave space to return and add keys you find as you continue your journey. These could be words to remember, ideas to revisit, or practical steps to take that apply these concepts.

CREATIVITY KEY

_____

_____

CREATIVITY KEY

_____

_____

CREATIVITY KEY

_____

_____

 **CREATIVITY GUIDE CORNER – Warning Light Awareness**
Personal reflections to consider. Follow @one.step.growth for more.

Becoming more aware of my own warning lights has helped reduce the frequency of falling into ditches in multiple areas of life. I'm far from perfect, but I'm also able to embrace being in process far more than when I started. It's more fun to spend energy joyfully creating than digging out of a hole created by miniature or significant burnout, which remains possible for any of us. Make time to regularly look for signs that you might be running low in capacity or energy. For me, if I'm consistently staying up too late snacking, having less patience at work or at home, watching many hours of sports games, or starting to feel waves of negative thoughts toward myself, it's often an indication that change is needed. Over-dependence on a certain activity that provides security or joy can lead to pressure and rush. This is true of anything, even artistic expression or one's efforts to serve others.

Recognizing opportunities for heart-alive creativity throughout our lives can help increase capacity for adjustments. Times of rest or creating in a different expression can also fuel cross-pollination of ideas. Listening back to a song might spark innovative ideas for a business project. Or, a work meeting might provide insight or a moment for vulnerable connection around emotional or mental health. Seeing various parts of life as channels for diversifying how we create joy and meaning sustains wellness. It makes us less dependent on any specific one. No matter your story or passions, your creativity has multiple facets.

Chapter 15
LEGACY

Do you ever wrestle with the idea that your creativity doesn't matter? That's a lie. Discover the potential impact of your small creative choices every day. Apply keys that spark inspiration and lessen pressure.

KEY CONCEPTS
Creativity Unlocked – Chapter 15

The Tapestry of Human Creativity

People you never meet, in places and times far from your location and interests, can be impacted through your creative actions, whether big or small. Psychologist Lev Vygotsky believed that every expression adds to the larger picture. He wrote, "When we consider the phenomenon of collective creativity, which combines all these drops of individual creativity that frequently are insignificant in themselves, we readily understand that an enormous percentage of what has been created by humanity is a product of the anonymous collective creative work of unknown inventors."* Much that we experience today that has come from the risks and sacrifices of people whose names we'll never know. The journeys of those who crafted your coffeemaker, penned popular folk songs, or paved your commute to school were shaped by the contributions of many. Each was a living, breathing, significant human beings who chose to create. You, too, can have greater creative reach than you can see or quantify.

Your individual story is part of a much larger, multi-generational narrative that connects us all. Unlocking joy and connection via your creativity brings the richer colors of vibrancy and passion to the threads your life weaves into this tapestry. You do not have to feel responsible for the whole tapestry. You simply get to discover and play your part in the artful weaving of humanity. You are a part of mending broken, dimmer places into something beautiful, even if you don't get to see the ultimate finished work in your lifetime. What could a world gleaming with joy-filled, meaningful creativity and connection look like? This vision of legacy can inspire how we create each day.

The contributions of celebrated pioneers remain important, but what will transform the planet in ways yet unseen is the activation of expressions and connection in the multitudes. A significant aspect of your legacy comes from where you impact others. The people you support, champion, or engage with, even in small capacities, will release their own creative expressions that affect others, and so on. The depth of impact depends not just on what you create but also on how you create. The businesses you serve, the art you produce, the experiences you share may fade from human memory, but the excellence, love, and goodness they release can continue to bear fruit through the hearts and values of the people they touch. Don't underestimate the creative power of your words and your kindness. They can help people recognize, brighten, strengthen, or mend their threads and those around them.

The opportunities around you today, no matter how small or big, are the outflows of the dreams of those who came before. Your "yes" to life, to hope, to activating the creative capacity

*Source: Lev Semenovich Vygotsky. Journal of Russian and East European Psychology, Vol. 42, No. 1, January–February 2004, p. 7–97. Accessed Feburary 22, 2022.

you have, can seed experiences for future generations, whether or not you see them sprout. If you go back nine generations from your parents, more than a thousand people were involved in your making. You have 1,024 eighth great-grandparents to be exact. You might gravitate to individuals who stand out for positive or negative reasons—the greatest hero or villain who has contributed fame or shame to your lineage. However, the truth is that the small creative choices and sacrifices of many played a role in you existing and in the strengths and positive qualities you carry.

Finding an Authentic Experience of Legacy

The creative tapestry of humanity contains both magnificence and mess. Recognition of its imperfections is essential for authentic experiences of its goodness. It is important to both celebrate the beauty of the tapestry and understand where it has been imperfect, wrong, or unjust. Considering the generational aspects of creativity may bring up pain from past or present situations. Some of the traumatic experiences that your ancestors walked through may have had severe negative ramifications for their descendants that continue today, including cycles of poverty, predisposition to health challenges, and relational dysfunction. Pain begets pain, until healing intervenes. If considering the topic of legacy is difficult for you, know that you're not alone. You can apply this topic through the lens of your family by birth or through people who have been part of your creative journey. Where you can see goodness and love passed down through your lineage, celebrate those gifts and choices. Where you see the opposite, let those points inspire you to be a part of creating something different.

Without recognition of one's inherent value, grace-filled mindsets, and an approach rooted in longevity, emphasizing legacy can backfire. It can become a heavy burden to bear, something that adds pressure to your process or dredges up regret. The keys throughout this workbook are designed to support a life-giving approach to legacy that increases inspiration and purpose. Remember: creativity thrives in freedom, not in fear or control. Take note if you start feeling the pressure to have or maintain a certain outflow or long-lasting impact. That can start choking out the delight of the process and ultimately lead to decisions rooted in fear that sour or dim the influence we have.

Every day, your life holds opportunities to add beauty to the spaces around you. Creating with delight and connection at home, in the workplace, or via other activities will bless your journey and overflow into others'. It's the conversation you have with a stranger who looks like they are going through a tough time. It's the new thought pattern you build to see yourself with kindness that empowers healthier parenting. It's the organizational or business solution you develop that adds value to someone's life. It's a daily word of gratitude that adds light.

Connection, in all of its imperfect, messy process and forms, is what holds this tapestry together. There's another name for this quality: love. When your time here is done, the impact of your love will remain. But we cannot pass along what we first don't learn to receive. This is why connection is the secret sauce to flourishing creativity. We aren't designed to carry the load of creating alone. Keep looking for experiences of love and light that fuel your journey.

JOURNAL PROMPT
Creativity Unlocked - Chapter 15

RECOGNIZING CREATIVE LEGACY

There are many ways we can leave a mark. How does recognizing the tapestry of humanity inspire new perspectives about the impact of your creative actions? The questions below are designed to fuel fresh creative vision and joy for different parts of your journey. Use another page if you need more space.

Who is someone in your creative or family lineage who inspires you? Are there examples of creative legacy from which you have benefitted?

Where can you see how acts of kindness or generosity from others make possible what you're creating today?

What is a challenge in your family, community, or city that you want to create solutions for?

What qualities and values do you want to pass on to future generations? What kind of creative legacy do you dream about? Via hobbies? Work? Family?

What emotions does the concept of legacy evoke for you? If there are places of pressure or pain, what next steps can you take to lighten the burden or seek healing?

ACTIVATION EXERCISE
Creativity Unlocked - Chapter 15

MAKE A WAKE TODAY

The ripples from a stone spread far across the surface of a lake. Your acts of kindness can have a bigger impact than you think. Over the next four days, make time to broaden your wake by intentionally expressing encouragement or love to four different people. If possible, pair your words with a tangible act. Buy them a gift, help around their house, write a note. To narrow the possibilities, below are guidelines for picking the targets of your kindness. As you complete the tasks, write out what you did in the blanks below. Take note of how this exercise shifts your emotions, and feel free to repeat as often as you would like. Happy creating!

Create kindness for someone you know with a similar creative expression.

_____

_____

Create kindness for someone who is either a family member or a very close friend.

_____

_____

Create kindness for someone you <u>don't know personally</u> with a similar expression.

_____

_____

Create kindness for a stranger unrelated to a specific creative expression.

_____

_____

KEY COLLECTION ZONE

What ideas resonated with you most from this section? Use this space to record after your first reading and leave space to return and add keys you find as you continue your journey. These could be words to remember, ideas to revisit, or practical steps to take that apply these concepts.

CREATIVITY KEY

_____

_____

CREATIVITY KEY

_____

_____

CREATIVITY KEY

_____

_____

CREATIVITY GUIDE CORNER – The Best Mark to Leave
Personal reflections to consider. Follow @one.step.growth on social media for more.

Some of your smallest creative acts may be the most impactful ones. An encouraging word to a friend in a crucial moment. Timely financial contributions to an organization, family member, or artist that sustains their journey. An introduction of marriage or business partners. In *Creativity Unlocked,* I recount the interwoven stories of a teacher, a professor, a public official, and a scientist whose connections over the span of decades helped spark innovations in farming that saved an estimated 1 billion lives. Recognizing the value of small creative acts rooted in connection can help fuel pursuit of bigger, longer-term dreams.

In a world focused on external validation, there can be unhealthy pressure to make a mark. Many people, myself included, have mixed a healthy desire for impact or success with a lack of identity and self-worth that translates into a constant need to prove oneself or justify one's existence. We don't realize how valuable and loved we already are. This can hurt personal wellness, diminish collaboration or openness to growth, and motivate unhealthy coping. Education, resources, and privilege can add to an unrecognized shame and feeling like one is constantly not doing enough. For me, the connection I experienced when I got sober empowered me to let go of this weight, deepen a sense of innate value, and re-engage with impact in a healthier way. Creativity and connection both thrive in freedom. The freedom from the need to have a legacy is the perfect place from which to create one.

A FINAL ENCOURAGEMENT

A Journey to Savor

Whew. Take a second to pause and celebrate what you've experienced over the last fifteen chapters. You have strengthened understanding of your creative nature, discovered and activated expressions that bring intrinsic joy and satisfaction, and learned about healing in places where shame and pain have hindered your process. You have received an invitation to explore narratives and discover outflows that make your heart alive in everyday life. You have upgraded mindsets, explored new approaches to community and discovered the secret sauce of creativity: connection. That is a lot, and you deserve a pat on the back.

As you continue to explore, refine, and share your creativity, keep in mind what helps you stay rooted in a childlike approach that prioritizes joy and authenticity, especially as you engage with external feedback and audiences. Don't be afraid to reach out for help if you get stuck. You have permission to remain curious and exploratory. As you progress and evolve, your creativity can flow from the joy and meaningful connection that you have been unlocking through this workbook. Allow the natural, emotional, and intangible inputs that inspire you to nourish your work, conversations, art, and adventures. You are designed to be a refreshing, life-supporting stream, not a stagnant pond. The more we experience the creative goodness of our expressions, the more we have to give away. But even before a choice to be generous, you have a choice to receive. Connection. Acceptance. Stories that inspire you.

Resist the temptation to be distracted by what others are doing or stymied by what you are lacking. There is a unique opportunity in your hands. Pick up the brush, the hammer, the phone, the map again. And again. And again. As you create, take time to rest and refresh the colors you release. Continue your healing journey, stepping into wholeness in places that have felt limited. Seek out deeper and resonant forms of connection as seasons change. Then keep hammering away at problems that waylay or confound with the chisel you carry . There is a role that is uniquely yours and beautiful in a story that stretches beyond what you can see. It's not too late to start afresh, even if you have tried before. Places of past failure and pain can become the starting point or very location of great redemption, beauty, and victory.

Embracing the passions of your heart gives permission for those around you to do the same. Whether you sense them now or not, the eyes of others will observe your healing, your growth, and your creative progress. Your dreams and hoped-for plans can be suddenly interrupted or delayed, but that can't erase the love released through the process. There is so much that we cannot control in this constantly changing world. But we can make the choice to keep showing up and to pursue deeper connection on every level that fuels both what we create and how we do so. Your creativity is powerful. The world is your canvas; your daily activities are your brushes. Love, kindness, and generosity are amongst your colors. What will you paint today?

CONTINUE YOUR CREATIVITY JOURNEY

BUY CREATIVITY UNLOCKED BOOK OR AUDIOBOOK

Enjoy more insights and encouragement, dozens of stories of individuals unlocking their creative nature, and deeper exploration of the topics in this workbook. Available in Kindle, print, or audiobook formats at Amazon or Barnes and Noble online, or email creativity@onestepguides.com

TAKE PART IN A CREATIVITY UNLOCKED WORKSHOP

Join a online cohort that provides personalized support and feedback for your creative journeys. Or learn about how to bring a customized version to your organization or business.

Visit www.onestepgrowth.com/creativity-workshop

GET THE CREATIVITY UNLOCKED APP

Access e-courses, daily encouragements, and dive deeper with tools that help you activate your creativity. Join for regularr challenges that help increase joy and connection in everyday life.

Questions or issues? Email creativity@onestepguides.com or visit creativity-unlocked.passion.io.

ONESTEP GROWTH

www.onestepgrowth.com

EXTRA CREATIVE SPACE
What will you create today?

Use the lines below to journal, complete exercises, brainstorm, or whatever you want.

EXTRA CREATIVE SPACE
What will you create today?

Use the lines below to journal, complete exercises, brainstorm, or whatever you want.

EXTRA CREATIVE SPACE
What will you create today?

Use the lines below to journal, complete exercises, brainstorm, or whatever you want.

EXTRA CREATIVE SPACE
What will you create today?

Use the lines below to journal, complete exercises, brainstorm, or whatever you want.